Korea and the Fall of MacArthur

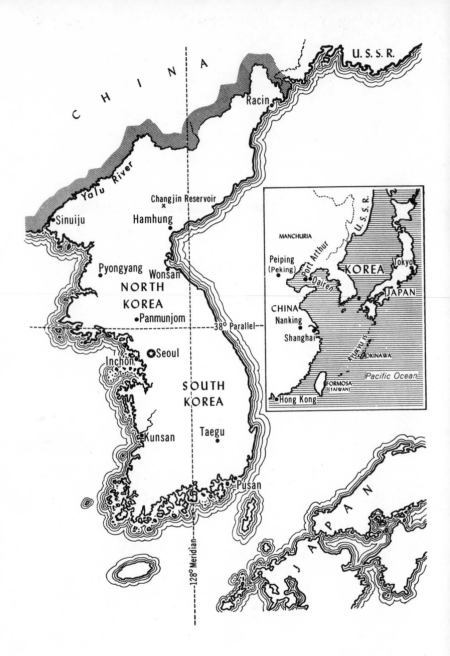

KOREA and the
Fall of MacARTHUR

A PRÉCIS IN LIMITED WAR

Trumbull Higgins

Oxford University Press New York

TO THOSE WHO REACH CONCLUSIONS

'A drama is about to begin which will be played by states-man and soldier in concert. . . . So closely interwoven is their dialogue that nothing said by either has any relevance, point or effect except with reference to the other. If one of them misses his cue, then disaster overwhelms them both.' [1]

—Charles de Gaulle

'When foreign affairs were ruled by autocracies or oli-garchies the danger of war was in sinister purpose. When foreign affairs are ruled by democracies the danger of war will be in mistaken beliefs.' [2]

—Elihu Root

'Appearance is not reality. War appears all the more "war-like" the deeper its political essence; and it appears all the more "political" the shallower its political essence.' [3]

—Marginal note of Lenin on Clausewitz

'I maintain that in war you must either trust your general or sack him.' [4]

—Field Marshal Sir John Dill

Preface

One of the most difficult problems facing the historian is how to withdraw from many of the basic assumptions of his time and place so that he can regard intensely controversial issues with the advantages of an outsider. Nevertheless—as the author discovered in his examination of Winston Churchill as a strategist—the historian actually has little choice in such a withdrawal. The fundamental assumptions of the principal parties to certain great disputes are often so utterly opposed that, for example, an orthodox conclusion, such as that victory is not the sole prerogative of the soldier, is likely to infuriate the military. Similarly, the pacifist, and much of the Left, may find fault with the essential desire of the professional soldier to win his war.

It must be recognized that the historian is not likely to alter the most profound convictions of men; such is not his intention. But the reader must understand that to both the protagonists in the dispute between General Mac-Arthur and the Truman Administration and to their analysts, one party's success constitutes the other's failure, one man's objectivity is necessarily another's bias.

In this connection the modest candor of Gaetano Salvemini may be recalled. In exile in 1931, Salvemini wrote: 'We cannot be impartial, we can only be intellectually honest—that is, aware of our own passions, on our guard against them, and prepared to warn the reader of the dangers into which our partial views may lead them. Impartiality is a dream, and honesty a duty.' [5]

It goes without saying that the nature of the Korean War has accentuated enormously the controversy between the Truman Administration and General MacArthur. Indeed, with the passage of time the war itself has become the focus of contemporary debate. In the well-chosen words of Irving Kristol: 'The problem can be stated simply. The Korean War was the most unpopular war in our history; and one reason lay in the fact that it was a limited war—limited in its scope and also limited in terms of popular participation. It was not a war that mobilized the emotional and physical energies of the entire American people. Not only was it a limited war; it was a most peculiar kind of limited war. It was an undeclared war against an unidentified enemy. Its aims were generally uncomprehended, possibly because they were never adequately explained by the Truman Administration. And the conduct of the war was as equivocal as its purpose.' [6]

The author wishes to acknowledge the unstinting aid of the many officers, journalists and historians who have made this work possible. He wants, also, to express his particular indebtedness to the Social Science Research Council for a fellowship, to the Woodrow Wilson School at Princeton University, to the Institute of War and Peace at Columbia University, and to the Defense Studies Program at Harvard University.

Grateful acknowledgment is made to the following publishers and individuals for permission to quote or reprint from their publications: The Council on Foreign Relations, *Korea: A Study of U.S. Policy in the United Nations* by Leland M. Goodrich (New York, 1956); Criterion Books, Inc., *The Edge of the Sword* by Charles de Gaulle (New

York, 196o); Dodd, Mead and Company, *Syngman Rhee, The Man Behind the Myth* by Robert T. Oliver, copyright by Robert T. Oliver (New York, 1954); Doubleday and Company, *Memoirs by Harry S. Truman,* Vol. II, *Years of Trial and Hope* (copr. 1956, Time Inc., New York); Harper and Brothers, *Calculated Risk* by Gen. Mark W. Clark (New York, 1950), and *Soldier: The Memoirs of Matthew B. Ridgway* (New York, 1956); Houghton Mifflin Company, *The Hinge of Fate* by Winston Churchill (Boston, 1950); Alfred A. Knopf, Inc., *MacArthur, His Rendezvous with History* by Maj. Gen. Courtney Whitney (New York, 1956); Lawrence and Wishart, Ltd., *Selected Works of Mao Tse-tung* (London, 1954); McGraw-Hill Book Company, Inc., *MacArthur: 1941-1951* by Maj. Gen. Charles Willoughby and John Chamberlain (New York, 1954); Princeton University Press, *Realities of American Foreign Policy* by George F. Kennan (Princeton, 1954); The United States Naval Institute, *The Sea War in Korea* by Comdr. M. C. Cagle and Comdr. F. A. Manson (Annapolis, 1957).

T. H.

June 1, 1960.
Washington, D.C.

Contents

Korea and the Fall of MacArthur

The Anticipations

1945 — 1950

'You think it is important that I have kept the Japanese from expanding . . . I tell you it is more important that I have kept the Communists from spreading. The Japanese are a disease of the skin; the Communists are a disease of the heart.' [1]

—Attributed to Chiang Kai-shek in 1941

'The secrets of our weakness are secrets only to our own people.' [2]

—Douglas MacArthur in 1934

'We can be certain that the next war, if there is one, will be even more total than this one. The nature of war is such that once it begins it can end only as this one is ending, in the destruction of the vanquished . . .' [3]

—Gen. George C. Marshall in 1945

'America's people expect you to be on a communing level with God and Joseph Stalin and I am not sure they are so much interested in God. They expect you to be able to say that a war will start next Tuesday at 5:32 P.M.' [4]

—Gen. Walter Bedell Smith in 1950

On AUGUST 15, 1945, IN THE INSTRUCTIONS FOR his General Order #1, General Douglas MacArthur was told by President Truman and the Joint Chiefs of Staff to accept as a matter of administrative convenience the surrender of all Japanese forces south of the 38th parallel in Korea. Although from Moscow, United States Ambassadors W. Averell Harriman and Edwin W. Pauley had urged the American occupation of as much of Korea and Manchuria as possible, on August 11 the Joint Chiefs of Staff had informed the Secretary of State, James F. Byrnes, that the United States would do well if it obtained even a foothold in southern Korea at Pusan in the event of a race into the peninsula with the Russians.[5]

Two months earlier at the Potsdam Conference the U.S. Army had turned down Soviet requests for a joint amphibious operation against Korea on the grounds that the then projected American invasion of Japan would require all available United States amphibious resources. When the Japanese surrender relieved enough landing craft to sustain the movement of a single American regiment into Korea, General MacArthur was willing to risk so small a force because of the Japanese desire to surrender to the Americans rather than to the rapidly advancing Russian forces. At the same time MacArthur refused to release seven U.S. infantry divisions from his command to strengthen the American position in North China, as was proposed at this juncture by the American Commander in China, Lt. Gen. Albert C. Wedemeyer. MacArthur did not expect the Japanese would be as docile as they proved and consequently had wished to retain his land forces for

5

what, in the last analysis hereafter, would always be conceived as his primary mission, the occupation and protection of Japan.[6]

Several months earlier, in February 1945, MacArthur had been resigned to the loss to Communism of all Manchuria and Korea and, perhaps, of North China, as 'inevitable,' and his opinions do not seem to have altered much at the moment when the United States first became the unwitting heir of Japan's imperial problems. Apart from a natural desire to obtain Soviet assistance during his then contemplated invasion of Japan,[7] this was also a normal logistic judgment for this period. By November 1945, however, MacArthur would tell the Chief of the Imperial General Staff, Sir Alan Brooke, that Russian expansion should be met by force, if necessary, although he was still resigned to the loss of North China to Communist influence.[8]

As it turned out, when the first regiment of the U.S. Army XXIV Corps finally managed to land in Korea on September 8-9, 1945, the Russian troops already occupying Inchon and Seoul, the Korean capital, retired north of the 38th parallel without apparent objection.[9] From its inception the 38th parallel would manifest a more durable character than its legal alternatives, since, like so many temporary military demarcations, it was firmly based on logistic reality.

By May 1947, demobilization of the United States armed forces had reached a point where the Secretary of War, Robert P. Patterson, would urge the State Department to consider an American withdrawal from Korea, both because a tighter Army budget could not stand the expense of the occupation and because of Korea's relative strategic insignificance.[10] Although not in agreement with

6

Patterson, the Secretary of State, George Catlett Marshall, former Chief of Staff of the U.S. Army, was himself painfully aware of the swift diminution of American military strength. Subsequently he would testify that in the period before 1950 the U.S. Joint Chiefs even found it difficult to obtain enough men to guard airstrips in Alaska, while the U.S. occupation garrison in Japan was set at only 60 per cent of strength.[11] Not surprisingly under these circumstances, by the fall of 1947 Secretary Marshall likewise was giving his most serious thought to the problem of how the United States could get out of Korea 'without loss of face.'[12] This did not promise to be easy, since the American commander in Korea, Lt. Gen. John R. Hodge, had recently emphasized that an American withdrawal in 1947 would mean the North Korean or Communist dominance of the whole peninsula.[13]

To avoid such an outcome, in a subsequently controversial confidential report made at the request of President Truman in September 1947, Gen. Albert C. Wedemeyer recommended not only a simultaneous Russian and American evacuation of Korea, but also that prior to such a joint withdrawal the United States should organize and equip a South Korean military force similar to the Philippine Constabulary and adequate in strength to resist the 'potential military threat' of the Communist-led North Koreans. Without such American assistance General Wedemeyer predicted a North Korean occupation of the whole peninsula by the 'vastly superior' Communist forces.[14]

In the light of the Wedemeyer report, on September 25, 1947, the Joint Chiefs of Staff—at that time consisting of Fleet Admirals Leahy and Nimitz and Generals Eisenhower and Spaatz—recommended to Secretary of State Marshall, in part, as follows:

7

The Joint Chiefs of Staff consider that, from the standpoint of military security, the United States has little strategic interest in maintaining the present troops and bases in Korea for the reasons hereafter stated.

In the event of hostilities in the Far East, our present forces in Korea would be a military liability and could not be maintained there without substantial reinforcement prior to the initiation of hostilities. Moreover, any offensive operation the United States might wish to conduct on the Asiatic continent most probably would by-pass the Korean peninsula.

If, on the other hand, an enemy were able to establish and maintain strong air and naval bases in the Korean peninsula, he might be able to interfere with United States communications and operations in East China, Manchuria, the Yellow Sea, Sea of Japan and adjacent islands. Such interference would require an enemy to maintain substantial air and naval forces in an area where they would be subject to neutralization by air action. Neutralization by air action would be more feasible and less costly than large-scale ground operations.

In the light of the present severe shortage of military manpower, the corps of two divisions, totaling some 45,000 men, now maintained in South Korea, could well be used elsewhere, the withdrawal of these forces from Korea would not impair the military position of the Far East Command unless, in consequence, the Soviets establish military strength in South Korea capable of mounting an assault on Japan.[15]

In October 1947 the United States proposed to the United Nations General Assembly a withdrawal of all foreign troops in Korea. This resolution was adopted by the Assembly in November 1947 and thereafter approved both by the U.S. Joint Chiefs of Staff and by General MacArthur.[16]

Shortly after the actual American troop withdrawal from

Korea had commenced in September 1948, disorders in South Korea among the Korean Constabulary provoked the Korean National Assembly to request a further delay in the retirement of the U.S. Army. At the urgent request of the State Department, now headed by Dean Acheson, an American regimental combat team was left in Korea until the late spring of 1949. Thus the last American troops did not depart until June 29, 1949, fully six months after the Soviet Union had announced the official departure of the Red Army from Korea.[17]

Debate regarding the condition of the South Korean forces left behind by the Americans has gone on for several years. Perhaps the most famous and unfortunate statement on this issue was uttered by Gen. William Roberts, head of the U.S. Military Aid Group to Korea. Shortly before the North Korean attack in June 1950, General Roberts said the South Korean forces included 'the best doggoned shooting army outside the United States.'[18] Following the abrupt South Korean collapse General Roberts would again embarrass the Administration when he declared that the South Korean Army had not been adequately armed because of an American fear that were this to be done the South Koreans would attack North Korea.[19]

A year earlier, in March 1949, before the final withdrawal of U.S. troops, the National Security Council had considered a MacArthur report to the effect that the training and combat readiness of the South Korean Army had reached a level which justified the U.S. Army's departure from the peninsula. Only two months later, however, in May 1949, Syngman Rhee, President of the Korean Republic, said: 'Whether the American soldiers go or stay does not matter very much. What is important is the policy of the United States towards the security of Korea.

9

What I want is a statement by President Truman that the United States would consider an attack against South Korea to be the same as an attack against itself.' And in June 1949 Rhee wrote: 'The American forces will be out of Korea by the end of this month. What do we do for our defense? Most of our Army men are without rifles and so is our police and Navy. Our defense minister reports that we have munitions which will last for only three days of actual fighting. . . . It is highly probable that if we explain this situation in some judicious and convincing manner, the American people may understand what we need and help us get it.' [20]

In retrospect, in 1951, General MacArthur largely repudiated the conclusions that the Truman Administration drew from his report of March 1949.[21] In 1951 the General also declared that it was a mistake to have pulled the American forces out of Korea, a position in implicit disagreement with Secretary Acheson, who at that time still found it somewhat more desirable to justify the American evacuation.[22]

During the Presidential campaign in 1952, Secretary Acheson was criticized by Dwight D. Eisenhower for having agreed (with a Republican senator) in March 1950 that the South Koreans could probably defend themselves against an attack from North Korea.[23] Acheson may have been relying here upon a much more positive affirmation of faith in the South Korean forces made in June 1949 by Maj. Gen. Charles Bolte, Director of the Plans and Operations Division of the U.S. Army General Staff. In June 1949 the U.S. Army had professedly feared the trap of another Bataan on the Korean peninsula in the event of an all-out Russian intervention in a Far Eastern war.[24] And in all probability in December 1949 the National Security

Council had decided against making any American response with ground troops in South Korea if there were a Communist invasion.[25] In a period when George F. Kennan, head of the State Department Policy Planning Staff, had failed to convince the Administration of the need for two Army divisions to cope with the possibility of a limited war in Europe, Korea was a most dispensable luxury, whatever might be argued both before and after the American decision to intervene.[26]

In 1954, General MacArthur's former intelligence chief, Maj. Gen. Charles A. Willoughby, wrote that what he termed the 'inexplicable decision' to equip the South Korean army as a constabulary rather than as a combat force was made in Washington without consulting MacArthur's headquarters—a headquarters which purportedly disapproved of this decision. Two years later, in 1956, General MacArthur himself said that he had recommended the departure of the U.S. Army from Korea only on the basis of the creation of a well-armed and full-strength South Korean force of ten divisions.[27]

MacArthur's command, of course, was not responsible for Korea in 1949, since by this period the peninsula was under the jurisdiction of the State Department. According to Secretary Marshall the State Department also could not build up effective Korean forces, because South Korea was now an independent nation no longer under United States control.[28] Moreover, in 1949-50 many Republicans in Congress were strongly resisting appropriations for South Korean aid and could be induced to accept such appropriations only when they were coupled with assistance for Nationalist China.[29]

At the same time the situation in Korea was fairly well recognized by certain members of Congress. In July 1949

it was stated in a House Minority Report: 'Our forces ...
have been withdrawn from South Korea at the very instant
when logic and common sense both demanded no retreat
from the realities of the situation. . . . Our position is
untenable and indefensible.' [30] And in 1949 Republican
Representative Judd of Minnesota charged that the Administration's Korean aid program was no more than 'an
attempt to make the Koreans and the world think that we
are carrying out a commitment which we are not prepared
to carry out.' With disturbing accuracy Judd predicted
that if the United States removed all its forces from
Korea, the Communists would probably take over the
whole peninsula within a year. [31]

Following the North Korean assault all American authorities agree that the South Korean Army was lacking
in tanks, artillery of all calibers, and combat planes, although how much difference this made, given its poor leadership, training, and morale, is open to question. [32] Possibly
the best explanation for the widespread American confusion on the question of the military capacities of the South
Koreans may be found in the opinion of Gen. Omar
Bradley, the Chairman of the Joint Chiefs of Staff, that in
June 1950 few Americans had recognized that the North
Koreans were so strong. Here the rapid build-up of the
North Korean Army in the spring of 1950 [33] may have con-
tributed to misleading the United States.

Another source of future acrimonious debate involved
the status of Formosa, even before the Korean War broke
out. Here again General MacArthur and some of his critics
of the future were in initial agreement, little as each may
have been inclined to recall this after circumstances had
changed. For example, twice during 1949 in interviews
with journalists General MacArthur outlined a U.S. de-

fense perimeter which clearly excluded Formosa.[34] Likewise in August 1949, the Joint Chiefs of Staff reaffirmed their earlier view that the United States should not forcibly prevent a Chinese Communist assault on Formosa, although the Joint Chiefs were concerned over the political and, perhaps, even the military effect of the fall of Formosa on the areas within the United States defense perimeter.[35] In September 1949 the Joint Chiefs turned down a proposal to send a U.S. Military Mission to Formosa, a position which they reaffirmed in December 1949.[36]

During 1949 the State Department foresaw the 'probability of the fall' of Formosa in 1950, as, indeed, had the Joint Chiefs of Staff until the end of 1949. In December 1949 the Joint Chiefs became less certain of an imminent Communist invasion of Formosa and recommended a modest program of military aid for this last refuge of the Chinese Nationalist Government.[37] The State Department, more pessimistic, went on preparing public opinion for the still anticipated fall of Formosa. A difference of judgment between the J.C.S. and the State Department was now appearing; General Bradley felt that Formosa had some strategic significance, but in a confidential bulletin on December 23, 1949, the State Department, in effect, denied any such significance. The conflict was temporarily resolved when after the speech of President Truman on January 5, 1950, opposing military aid to Formosa, the Joint Chiefs dropped the subject.[38] Sensing a rare opportunity for political gain, and spurred by a leak from General MacArthur's headquarters regarding the Administration decision, the Republicans in Congress did not.[39]

Most unfortunately for a policy of calculated ambiguity in this area, in a famous speech before the National Press

13

Club on January 12, 1950, Secretary of State Acheson officially spelled out the new American defense perimeter in the Far East. Korea, and still more Formosa, were beyond the pale, areas where, in Mr. Acheson's significantly awkward phrase, American guarantees were neither 'sensible or necessary within the realm of practical relationship.' Acheson did concede, however, that to some extent the United States still had a direct responsibility for Korea, although nothing like its commitment to Japan. While the Secretary of State affirmed that the United States would continue to resist aggression beyond its defense perimeter under the aegis of the United Nations,[40] both Formosa and South Korea were legally no more than components of larger states whose unification under Communist auspices might well not provoke sanctions on the part of the United Nations.

Five months later, in May 1950, Senator Tom Connally, the Democratic Chairman of the Senate Foreign Relations Committee, went further than Mr. Acheson and publicly announced, in what was not always considered just his own opinion, that Russia could seize South Korea at her convenience and that the United States would probably not intervene, since Korea was not 'very greatly [sic] important.'[41] But in the middle of June, in a private discussion in Tokyo, General MacArthur and Defense Secretary Louis Johnson found themselves in agreement on the importance of Formosa.[42] Clearly the public diplomatic and private military policies of the United States had not been reconciled, which the Soviet Union could not be expected to know.

It is not unreasonable to conclude with Dwight D. Eisenhower or Robert A. Taft that the Truman Administration had thus convinced the Communists that the

United States would not defend South Korea—or for that matter Formosa—against indigenous Asian Communist aggression.[43] On the other hand it is possible to sympathize with Secretary Acheson's somewhat undiplomatic desire to differentiate publicly between the few vital places which the United States might have the strength to defend and those 'many, many places where it is very desirable that they should be kept out of hostile hands [but] where we do not have a policy to commit [American] troops.'[44]

On the much bruited issue of the warnings received by the United States before the North Korean attack on June 24 the argument has chiefly revolved about efforts by the authorities in Washington and those in Tokyo to reveal the faults or inadequacies of each other's intelligence. Certainly General MacArthur's G-2 section received a vast quantity of information regarding Korea, although this country was not strictly within MacArthur's orbit of responsibility. For example, in September 1949 MacArthur's headquarters noted Chinese Communist troops of Korean descent were entering North Korea in great numbers since the end of the Chinese civil war on the Asian mainland had essentially been achieved. In December 1949 and January 1950 Tokyo learned that the threat of the well-equipped North Korean Army to South Korea would become more pronounced in the more favorable weather of the spring of 1950. In a notable dispatch from Tokyo to Washington on March 10, 1950, rumors of an impending North Korean assault in June 1950 were reported, but two weeks later the G-2 of the U.S. Far East Command had concluded that there would be no civil war in Korea in the spring or summer of that year.[45]

By June, notwithstanding anxiety concerning attack in South Korea, the American authorities in Seoul, Tokyo, and Washington were in agreement that while a North Korean offensive was possible it was not imminent. Certainly in Tokyo a few days before the Communist attack, Secretary of Defense Johnson and General Bradley received no advance warning regarding Korea from MacArthur's headquarters, although there was much concern regarding the supposed threat of Communist China to Formosa. At this time, in the opinion of various United States intelligence agencies, guerrilla and psychological methods of warfare seemed sufficiently profitable for the Communists in Korea.[46] As before Pearl Harbor,[47] Americans had become surfeited with misleading reports and had in any event refused to accept the probability of an all-out enemy attack; as in the Hawaiian Islands in 1941, internal subversion in South Korea was seemingly so much more persistent and dangerous.

Nevertheless, if miscalculations in both camps [48] helped to precipitate the Korean War, in retrospect, at least, the Communist error appears to have been more excusable, although less innocent, than the American. Neither in Moscow nor in Pyongyang, the North Korean capital, may the significance of a speech by John Foster Dulles have been fully appreciated until it was too late. On June 17, 1950, in Seoul as a special envoy, Mr. Dulles personally assured the [South] Korean National Assembly that the American people remained 'faithful to the cause of human freedom and loyal to those everywhere who honorably support it!' Upon concluding, Mr. Dulles reiterated on a more Republican note as far as the Asia mainland was then concerned: 'You are not alone; you will never be alone, as long as you continue to play worthily your part in the great design of human freedom.' [49]

As the Communists were about to discover, the danger

with ideals is that sometimes others, too, have to uphold them in practice. And, as Americans were about to learn once again, even abortive crusades launched for high moral ends cannot be easily arrested short of total victory, regardless of how that popular objective may be defined.

The Choice

June 1950

'The theory was widely held at the beginning of the Mediterranean campaign that the German armies could not fight effectively in Italy. It was believed that our superior air power could quickly destroy the enemy's supply lines through the Alpine passes and down the long, mountainous spinal column of Italy, and that, being unable to maintain himself logistically, he soon would find it unprofitable if not impossible to give battle.

'This was wishful thinking.' [1]

—Gen. Mark Clark

'The Cabinet was encouraged to believe that Nasser might be destroyed by the bombing alone, and that, in a favorite phrase of the R.A.F., it would not be necessary to "land the pongos." This delectable carrot excited the political appetite of some members of the Cabinet, and made them think that they might achieve their objective without becoming involved in any land operations.' [2]

—Randolph Churchill

'The great error of nearly all studies of war . . . has been to consider war as an episode in foreign policies, when it is especially an act of interior politics, and the most atrocious act of all.' [3]

—Simone Weil

'This is the Greece of the Far East. If we are tough enough now, there won't be any next step.' [4]

—Harry S. Truman, June 26, 1950

On JUNE 25, ONE DAY AFTER THE NORTH Korean offensive had commenced, as a consequence of the Soviet boycott of its sessions the United Nations Security Council was able to call on the North Korean forces to retire behind the 38th parallel. This United Nations action enabled Secretary Acheson on June 26 to support American action in accord with the U.N. resolution, without thus appearing to have altered fundamentally United States policy. Later on Mr. Acheson would carefully explain that a United Nations action to repel aggression was 'not a question of a war between the United States and some other country,' a policy which, indeed, so far as Korea was concerned, Acheson had vigorously repudiated in his speech of January 12, 1950.[5]

The Administration's neutralization of the Formosa Straits at this time against action in either direction by Chinese Nationalists or Chinese Communists similarly reflected its unwillingness to go over fully to a neo-isolationist Republican policy of a private American war in the Far East. The Administration's action appears to have been evoked, in part, by a report brought back from Tokyo by Defense Secretary Louis Johnson on his trip to the Far East in mid-June 1950. This report, stemming from General MacArthur's headquarters, had stressed a rapid Chinese Communist build-up on the mainland opposite Formosa. In 1951 Johnson would assert that it was his influence which had induced the momentarily reluctant Secretary of State, Dean Acheson, to accept the neutralization of the Formosa Straits.[6]

In common with its political chiefs the principal military figures associated with the Truman Administration now abruptly agreed that Korea was a necessary point at which to stop further Communist aggression in the Far East, although in General Bradley's words the peninsula still was not 'part of the strategic long-range defense' pattern. General Bradley would subsequently explain that the United States was trying to prevent a third world war by fighting a limited war in Korea.[7]

Henceforth this would constitute the essence of the Administration's policy toward Korea. As Robert Osgood has put it, the Truman Administration was 'tacitly following the imperatives of the strategy of containment, [imperatives] which had been excluded from over-all strategic planning by virtue of the prevailing political blindness and preoccupation with total war.'[8] The Administration's refusal to declare war officially was—to employ its strikingly ineffective euphemism of the time—an aspect of its determination to fight no more than as limited a police action as possible.[9]

From the beginning of the Korean War this was probably what had most disturbed the Republican leader, Senator Robert Taft. In his speech of June 28, reluctantly accepting the Administration's decision on Korea—and the Senator could hardly have opposed the Administration action in view of his previous attitude—Taft nevertheless damned the Democrats both for having invited the attack and for fighting a war without Congressional concurrence. In a marvelous reflection of Republican isolationist and nationalist ambivalence the Senator also blamed the Administration for completely changing its Asian policy 'at an unfortunate time.'[10] It is questionable whether any overseas war undertaken at any time by the Truman Administration would have ever won Senator Taft's unqualified support—even one in the Far East.

In June 1950, however, many Republicans were more positive regarding an American intervention in Korea. On the day of the Communist attack, June 25th, Senator Alexander Smith of New Jersey declared that the United States had a 'moral responsibility' toward the 'infant' South Korean republic. After the now customary Republican assertion that the whole problem had resulted from the Administration's China policy, Senator Kenneth Wherry, from isolationist Nebraska, concluded that the United States 'should stand up and do something and then we'll stop these Commies.' [11] On June 27th Senator William Knowland of California, a great admirer of Nationalist China, said: 'If Korea is not supported and maintained, there is no place on the continent of Asia that can be ultimately supported and maintained.' [12] And regardless of his subsequent attitudes, on this occasion John Foster Dulles favored upholding the moral posture which he had so recently proclaimed in Seoul.[13]

Furthermore, if Secretary of Defense Johnson has stressed the excessively flagrant character of the North Korean assault as the principal reason for the reversal of the Administration's policy and its entry into the Korean War,[14] the Republican party's prolonged pressure on the Administration for being too soft on Communism in the Far East obviously also contributed to the Administration's fear of further loss of prestige should it fail to act. But having helped to saddle the Democrats with an unexpected and soon-to-be unpopular war in the Far East, the Republicans had no intention of relieving their political opponents of the onus of the war with the cloak of a bipartisan foreign policy.[15]

The role of the Joint Chiefs of Staff in this great decision seems largely to have been confined to discussions of the limits to be put on the war, and, particularly, whether or not Russia or Communist China might enter it. In June 1950 the J.C.S. doubted this last eventuality. Even the seemingly most lukewarm supporter of the Korean intervention, Adm. Forrest Sherman, considered the Korean War as 'unavoidable,' although as a naval officer he had grown up believing in not fighting Asians on their own continent. In August 1950 he would tell the Secretary of Defense that 'sooner or later, we should get out of the business of fighting on the Asiatic mainland.' [16] He would not be alone in those sentiments.

For example, among others, on June 28th, Mao Tse-tung made the following statement in an address in Peiping: 'The Chinese people have already affirmed that the affairs of the various countries throughout the world should be run by the peoples of these countries, and that the affairs of Asia should be run by the peoples of Asia and not by the United States. U.S. aggression in Asia will only arouse widespread and resolute resistance by the peoples of Asia. Truman stated on January 5 this year that the United States would not interfere in Taiwan [Formosa]. Now he has proved his own statement to be false.' [17]

On the still more important issue of the intentions of Soviet Russia, notwithstanding some bad moments, the Administration decided that Moscow would not directly intervene in Korea in response to the American action. After reading a somewhat ambiguous Russian reply to an American note of inquiry, with what appears to be remarkable insight President Truman is supposed to have remarked: 'That means that the Soviets are going to let the Chinese and North Koreans do the fighting for them.' [18]

The Administration's initial fear of an imminent general war would gradually be superseded by the suspicion that Korea constituted a deliberate Soviet diversion of American efforts from Europe.

General MacArthur and his headquarters in Tokyo were as surprised by the action of the United States and the United Nations in resisting the North Korean invasion as they had been by the enemy invasion itself. Evidently not consulted on these decisions, General MacArthur approved of them at the time, commenting only that they constituted a complete reversal of United States Far Eastern policy. A few weeks later, in rather more controversial language, MacArthur wrote to the Veterans of Foreign Wars that the Administration's decision 'swept aside in one great monumental stroke all the hypocrisy and the sophistry which has confused and deluded so many people distant from the actual scene.' [19] In the upshot, the Administration's decision also constituted, in MacArthur's phrase, ' "Mars" last gift to an old warrior' [20]—for his was the task of executing this remarkable reversal of United States governmental policy in the Far East.

General MacArthur's first order from Washington on June 25 consisted simply of instructions to employ United States sea and air power to evacuate American nationals from the Seoul area. At this juncture Gen. Hoyt Vandenberg, the Chief of Staff of the U.S. Air Force, and Admiral Sherman still hoped that United States air and sea power alone could enable the South Koreans to stop the Communist invasion. On the other hand, MacArthur's staff in Tokyo, more like Gen. J. Lawton Collins, the U.S. Army Chief of Staff, expected that all of Korea would be overrun within six weeks. Both the U.S. Army and Navy headquarters in Tokyo were then much concerned about the possibility of Russian intervention. The U.S. Navy commander in the area, Vice Adm. C. Turner Joy, promptly ordered the U.S. Seventh Fleet to proceed from the Philippines only to Okinawa because Japanese bases were too close to Soviet airfields.[21] If the U.S. Army had not forgotten Bataan, Pearl Harbor had not been effaced from the memory of the U.S. Navy.

On June 29 the Joint Chiefs of Staff directed MacArthur to use naval and air forces to support both South Korea and Formosa, but U.S. Army units were restricted to service functions except in a proposed beachhead at Pusan, the chief port of South Korea.[22] On June 30, following a perilous personal reconnaissance of the front lines in Korea, General MacArthur reported to the Joint Chiefs:

> The South Korean forces are in confusion, have not seriously fought, and lack leadership. Organized and equipped as a light force for maintenance of interior order, they are unprepared for attack by armor and air. Conversely they are incapable of gaining the initiative over such a force as that embodied in the North Korean Army. The South Koreans had made no preparation for defense in depth, for echelons of supply or for a supply system. No plans had been made, or if made were not executed, for the destruction of supplies or materials in the event of a retrograde movement. As a result they have either lost or abandoned their supplies and heavier equipment. . . .
>
> The only assurance for holding the present line and the ability to regain later the lost ground is through the introduction of United States ground combat forces into the Korean battle area. To continue to utilize the forces of our air and navy without an effective ground element cannot be decisive. If authorized it is my intention to immediately move a United States regimental combat team to the reinforcement of the vital area discussed and to provide for a possible

build-up to a two division strength from the troops in Japan for an early counteroffensive.

Unless provision is made for the full utilization of the Army-Navy-Air team in this shattered area, our mission will at best be needlessly costly in life, money and prestige. At worst, it might even be doomed to failure.[23]

If MacArthur was overly optimistic in his belief that two American divisions could turn the tide in Korea, there is little doubt his advice was most influential in evoking the final orders from the Joint Chiefs on June 30th to enter Korea with the U.S. Army in strength.[24] Some officials in Washington may have hoped that the simple commitment of United States ground troops would intimidate the enemy into halting, even after his attack had been launched.

Nevertheless MacArthur was far from sharing the conceit of a U.S. Air Force officer who, in criticizing MacArthur's call for ground troops, remarked: 'The old man must be off his rocker. When the Fifth Air Force gets to work on them, there will not be a North Korean left in North Korea.' Unfortunately, it soon enough became apparent that the U.S. Fifth Air Force was designed for the strategic air defense of Japan rather than a tactical offensive in Korea.[25] Finally, there was little time at this desperate juncture, either in Washington or in Tokyo, for second thoughts on all the implications of the American decision to use ground troops in Korea.

Regardless of pressure, in Washington, at least, one consideration was always kept foremost during these piece-meal decisions to enter Korea; this was President Truman's repeatedly expressed determination that he would not permit 'even the slightest implication' of any American intention to go to war with the Soviet Union over issues related to Korea. As early as June 29, before the final decision to intervene with the U.S. Army in force, Secretary of the Army Frank Pace had expressed similar views, stressing that the United States must be very careful to limit operations against the enemy in North Korean territory above the 38th parallel. The President then agreed to American actions to destroy enemy supplies above the parallel, so long as such operations were kept strictly within the borders of Korea.[26]

However, according to his aide, General MacArthur had already decided on such operations in North Korea quite independently of the Administration's almost simultaneous decision. In Maj. Gen. Courtney Whitney's enthusiastic language: 'Here was no timid delay while authorization was obtained from Washington; here was the capacity for command decision and the readiness to assume responsibility which had always been MacArthur's forte.'[27]

On another matter, President Truman was at first inclined to accept Generalissimo Chiang Kai-shek's politically astute offer on June 29 of 33,000 Chinese Nationalist troops for use in Korea. But Secretary of State Acheson opposed accepting this contribution on the grounds that Formosa was exposed to attack and that employment of Nationalist troops in Korea might provoke the Chinese Communists to intervene in Korea. The Joint Chiefs were also disinclined to accept Chiang's forces, since the Chinese Nationalists were then poorly equipped and American transport could be more profitably employed carrying better trained American troops to Korea. In addition, U.S. Army generals undoubtedly placed little faith in the morale of Chinese Nationalist troops in this period, and for the moment General MacArthur himself preferred American troops with which to face the mounting crisis in

Korea.[28] Thus the question of another restriction on Mac-Arthur's future intentions did not arise at this time.

Yet for better or worse the U.S. Army was now definitely re-established on the Asian mainland, and the United States was committed to a land war—a war, to be sure, rigidly restricted in geographic bounds, but of a most uncertain duration and outcome.

Land War and Preventive War

July — August 1950

'In no other profession are the penalties for employing un-trained personnel so appalling and so irrevocable as in the military.' [1]

—Douglas MacArthur in 1933

'There never is a convenient place to fight a war when the other man starts it.' [2]

—Adm. Arleigh Burke in 1958

'I do not desire to place myself in the most perilous of posi-tions, a fire upon my rear, from Washington, and the fire in front from the Mexicans.' [3]

—Gen. Winfield Scott in 1846

'I'll not be party to another Korea, and that is what the country is facing up to.' [4]

—Gen. James Gavin in 1958

On JULY 7, 1950, THE UNITED NATIONS ASKED the United States to designate an American commander for the United Nations forces in Korea. The next day President Truman announced General MacArthur's appointment in this capacity.[5]

Following his perception that 'determined ground troops cannot be stopped alone by air [action],' and that 'perhaps too much was expected of the air' by Americans, the first problem faced by General MacArthur in Korea in early July was to obtain ground troops as quickly as possible.[6] Apart from the disintegrating South Korean Army, the only forces immediately available to MacArthur lay in the four skeletonized American divisions garrisoning nearby Japan. Indeed, the proximity of one of the two largest American forces overseas would alone render possible an effective United States and United Nations intervention in Korea.

Of course, two of General MacArthur's staff officers, Generals Whitney and Willoughby, have explained that in this period too many American troops were being sent to Europe.[7] Nevertheless, the American garrison in Japan at this time was four divisions as opposed to two in Germany. Although his forces were approximately the same size in manpower as the American garrison in Europe, MacArthur, with commendable foresight, had insisted upon preserving the cadres of his four divisions for the sake of a speedier subsequent expansion of his forces, should this prove necessary. In the United States itself only one Army division and part of one Marine division were ready for immediate service, and these could not be shipped to Korea for some weeks.[8] Before the Korean War, the Chairman of the Joint Chiefs of Staff, Gen. Omar Bradley, had failed in an effort to maintain a larger ready reserve in the United States.[9]

More serious than the over-all inadequacy of American ground troops for limited war in June 1950 was the fact that General MacArthur's divisions in Japan required a thorough rebuilding, retraining, and re-equipping before they would be ready for combat with the well-led and fairly well-equipped North Korean Communists.[10] The days of automatic Western military superiority over Asians had departed, as French statesmen and generals were learning to their cost at this same time.

In fact, in spite of the doubts of the United States Eighth Army Commander, Lt. Gen. Walton Walker, Mac-Arthur would eventually be driven to bring his under-strength U.S. divisions to their full complements of manpower, both by cannibalizing one division for the benefit of the others and by incorporating discouraged and poorly led South Korean soldiers into the cannibalized U.S. 7th Division—this last a desperate expedient to which the U.S. Army in Korea had again been reduced by 1959, but one which paid off during the Inchon offensive in September 1950.[11] Matériel was a somewhat less serious problem, since American equipment was not much more than five years old [12]—the last war in which the United States had fought having most fortunately been concluded only in 1945. Nevertheless, American tanks and, to some extent, U.S. anti-tank weapons proved to be too light against Russian medium tanks. Since the American divisions from Japan had been originally designed as occupation troops, they were also short of field artillery. As Gen. Matthew Ridgway would put it, because of defense economies the condition (not to mention the morale) of the U.S. Army in Japan at the outbreak of the Korean War was inexcusable.[13]

On July 5 soldiers of the U.S. 24th Division first encountered the enemy in Korea, in what General MacArthur for once inadequately described as an 'arrogant display of strength.' The exposure of two battalions of this U.S. division, not to mention the over-exposure of its gallant commander, Maj. Gen. Dean, distracted the North Korean advance long enough for two more American divisions from Japan, the 25th Infantry and the 1st Cavalry, to disembark on beachheads at which the enemy was momentarily expected.[14] In the opinion of Lt. Gen. James Gavin, the absence of an airlift large enough to fly a major number of troops speedily into Korea was the most serious of all the many American inadequacies in fighting a limited war. According to Gavin and other Army leaders, the U.S. airlift was still inadequate in 1958.[15]

By July 19, when the stripping of his Japanese base of American troops for Korea was well under way, in a further bluff to confuse and delay the enemy, General MacArthur said that the North Korean bid for victory had failed, since the U.S. Eighth Army was now ashore in Korea in strength. And, in fact, MacArthur was already planning offensive operations against the enemy.[16]

During these events the question of Formosa refused to remain buried under the protection of the U.S. Seventh Fleet. In a statement on July 3, considered by President Truman as no more than a dangerous 'bluster,' Generalissimo Chiang Kai-shek asked the United Nations to condemn Moscow as fully responsible for the Korean War.[17]

At the same time, in a conference with the British Government, the Administration decided that no further risks

35

of extending the war in the Far East either to Communist China or Russia could be sustained without running too grave a danger of a general war. The U.S. Air Force was ordered not to make photo-reconnaissance flights beyond the Yalu River for fear, in the words of President Truman, that such flights might give the Soviet Union 'a pretext to come into open conflict with us.' [18] The issue of what would constitute provocation to Soviet Russia or Communist China would constantly face an Administration determined, at all costs, to avoid a general war.

By the end of the month, on July 27, under the influence of the U.S. Joint Chiefs of Staff, the Administration agreed to grant military aid to the Chinese Nationalists for the sake of building up their defensive positions on Formosa. MacArthur was ordered to survey the Chinese Nationalist military requirements, an order which he regarded as an opportunity to undertake a personal visit to Generalissimo Chiang Kai-shek on Formosa, despite a marked lack of enthusiasm on the part of the State Department for such an action. [19]

The Joint Chiefs of Staff and General MacArthur remained in agreement on the ineffectiveness of the Chinese Nationalist forces for offensive warfare in Korea. There, as General MacArthur wished to explain tactfully to Chiang Kai-shek, the United Nations already had too many poorly trained and equipped troops in the South Korean Army, and any additional numbers of such troops would create a logistic burden which the U.S. Army could not undertake at this time. [20]

Although long before his visit with Chiang Kai-shek on July 31 General MacArthur had favored releasing the Chinese Nationalists for raids along the Chinese coast to break up any impending Communist invasion, the General had the unpleasant task of explaining to Chiang that this also was forbidden by U.S. government policy. Nevertheless, the Generalissimo's suspiciously happy announcement on August 2, following MacArthur's visit, to the effect that 'the foundation for ... Sino-American military cooperation has been laid' upset both Washington [21] and London [22] with its vague connotations of an unlimited military alliance. Chiang's pointed remarks about the deep understanding of Communism displayed by his old 'comrade-in-arms,' Douglas MacArthur,[23] likewise left the implication that the government in Washington understood Communism rather less well. For Chiang an opportunity such as this to retaliate against a long series of Truman Administration rebuffs must have been sweet.

The distress, and indeed distrust, in Washington and London resulting from MacArthur's conversations with the Chinese Nationalists culminated in an official warning in early August to the effect that he must continue to prevent any Nationalist attack from Formosa on the Asian mainland. This directive of the Secretary of Defense concluded sharply: 'No one other than the President as Commander-in-Chief has the authority to order or authorize preventative action against concentrations on the mainland. ... the most vital national interest requires that no action of ours precipitates general war or gives excuse to others to do so.' [24]

With the issue of authority about to be so bluntly presented, General MacArthur's comment on August 5 is quite self-revealing. 'It is extraordinarily difficult,' he said, 'for me at times to exercise that degree of patience which is unquestionably demanded if the longtime policies which have been decreed are to be successfully accomplished without repercussions which would be detrimental to the well-being of the world, but I am restraining myself to the best of my ability and am generally satisfied with the progress being made.' [25]

Somewhat less satisfied with MacArthur's progress in diplomacy was an Administration representative, Mr. W. Averell Harriman, who arrived in Tokyo on August 6 to brief MacArthur further on the official line. Harriman left Tokyo still not certain that MacArthur agreed with the Administration on Formosa, but very well acquainted with the General's views on many other issues. These Harriman summarized as exceedingly aggressive toward Communism everywhere, although at the same time MacArthur did not believe that either the Russian or Chinese Communists had any intention of becoming involved in a general war. MacArthur wanted more Occidental soldiers in order to launch an early offensive against the North Koreans, and the General emphasized his opinion that time was of the essence, since the Russian and Chinese Communists would continue to strengthen the North Koreans. MacArthur also could not refrain from venturing into the political realm when he maintained that the United States was not improving its position 'by kicking Chiang around'; but he agreed as a soldier to obey the orders he received from the President. [26]

World-wide speculation regarding the significance of his trip to Formosa evoked a public statement from the General on August 10 to the effect that only military issues had been discussed in his conversation with Chiang Kai-shek. MacArthur's resentment over his private restrictions, however, came out in the final sentence of his explanation, when he declared that his visit to Chiang Kai-shek had been 'maliciously misrepresented to the public by those who invariably in the past have propagandized a policy of defeatism and appeasement in the Pacific.' [27] The Administration was again about to discover that even a private warning to MacArthur could be a dangerous business.

A week later, on August 17, General MacArthur received an invitation from the Veterans of Foreign Wars to send a message for their annual encampment. In his soon famous reply MacArthur argued that, among other Pacific outposts, Formosa must be held or otherwise 'war is inevitable.' In fact, most remarkably in view of his indifference toward this island during the Second World War, MacArthur suggested that the loss of Formosa would drive the United States five thousand miles back to the defense of its own Pacific coast. More to the point, since the Administration itself no longer dared to let Formosa fall, was MacArthur's often reiterated opinion that Oriental psychology could only 'respect and follow aggressive, resolute and dynamic leadership' in contrast with a 'leadership characterized by timidity or vacillation.' Few, except General MacArthur's aides,[28] have shown much doubt about the identity of those whom General MacArthur had in mind here.

Whether MacArthur chose to consider these opinions as 'purely . . . personal,' and as supporting governmental policy or not, the Truman Administration could hardly avoid considering this contemptuous characterization of its Asian policy, past and present, as a studied public insult.[29] Moreover, even before the appearance of MacArthur's message to the Veterans of Foreign Wars, Red Chinese threats as a result of his trip to Formosa [30] had dismayed an Administration so eager to avoid an extension of the conflict in the Far East.

When the President's attention was first brought to

MacArthur's message on August 26, two days before its formal release date, he immediately ordered the General to withdraw it. Unfortunately, since MacArthur's public relations officer in Tokyo had given the message to the press several days earlier, it was already too late to suppress it entirely, and the message appeared in two national American magazines. As Senator Wayne Morse later suggested, the message, therefore, had much the same effect as if it had been delivered in person.[31]

President Truman was so disturbed over the episode that, according to his own statement, for the first time he seriously considered relieving MacArthur of his command and replacing him with General Bradley. An additional factor at this time which probably fanned the President's anxiety on his seeming loss of control over American policy appeared with Secretary of the Navy Francis Matthews's speech of August 25, openly advocating a preventive war with Russia. But, like MacArthur, Matthews was not replaced either. Instead, a month later Secretary of Defense Louis Johnson, who, among several other more probable liabilities, may have also been suspected of favoring a preventive war, was asked to resign. The discreet and modest officer whom President Truman most admired in the armed services, Gen. George Marshall, stepped into Johnson's shoes.[32]

Like Abraham Lincoln, whom he resembled at least in courage, President Truman was biding his time and preparing for the future. Like Gen. George McClellan, Douglas MacArthur was already confusing his popularity as a symbol of patriotism in a nation at war with his duty as a general on active service.

IV

An Option of Difficulties

Summer 1950

'Experience shows me that in an affair depending upon vigor and dispatch, the Generals should settle their plan of operations, so that no time may be lost in idle debate and consultations when the sword should be drawn . . . that nothing is to be reckoned an obstacle to your undertaking which is not found readily so upon trial; that in war something must be allowed to chance and fortune, seeing it is in its nature hazardous, and an option of difficulties.' [1]

—Gen. James Wolfe

'Some operations which, if carried out to their logical end may change the entire aspect of war . . . The entire movable army strikes at the enemy in the heart of his own country. Such resolutions by great generals are stamped with the mark of true genius.' [2]

—Dennis Hart Mahan

'I am wondering whether we shall ever have another large-scale amphibious operation. Frankly, the atomic bomb, properly delivered, almost precludes such a possibility.' [3]

—Gen. Omar N. Bradley, October 19, 1949

'For your information, the Marine Corps is the Navy's police force and as long as I am President that is what it will remain. They have a propaganda machine that is almost equal to Stalin's.' [4]

—Harry S. Truman, August 29, 1950

GENERAL MacARTHUR'S DETERMINATION TO initiate an offensive had existed from the beginning of the Korean campaign, but it was not until early July that he began to perceive the means with which to realize his intention. On July 2 MacArthur learned from the U.S. Naval Commander in the Far East, Vice Adm. C. Turner Joy, of the availability of a Marine regiment for an amphibious operation. Obtaining the right to employ it from the Joint Chiefs on the next day, General MacArthur ordered planning to start for an almost immediate assault on the Inchon-Seoul area, the logistic heart of Korea. Unfortunately the need to reinforce the hard-pressed U.S. 24th Division in Korea with the bulk of his remaining garrison in Japan soon thwarted this ambitious project and on July 10 it was temporarily abandoned.[5]

At the same time MacArthur heard from Lt. Gen. Lemuel C. Shepherd, Commanding General of the Fleet Marine Force in the Pacific, that, if necessary, the whole 1st Marine Division could be delivered to the Far East within six weeks. From July 10 on MacArthur bombarded the Joint Chiefs with requests both for this fine Marine Division and for enough Army troops to build up his last American division in Japan for a new amphibious corps. Because of tidal conditions and the need to relieve General Walker's Eighth Army as soon as possible, MacArthur now ordered his unenthusiastic naval staff in Tokyo to consider September 15 as their target date. On July 15 he informed the J.C.S. that a decision on their part regarding the 1st Marine Division was urgent since the employment of this trained amphibious unit was 'absolutely essential to achieve a decisive stroke.' [6]

The Chief of Staff of the Army, Gen. J. Lawton Collins, in Korea at this time, was, perhaps, the most hesitant of the J.C.S. concerning the Inchon project. With Admiral Sherman he believed that the appalling tides at Inchon would be too severe and that the beaches there were inadequate for landings. Privately Collins preferred a less ambitious objective further south on the Korean west coast, an objective which would be easier to assault. In all probability the U.S. Army had not forgotten the last two-divisional amphibious assault which it had been induced by Winston Churchill to launch against the heart of another mountainous peninsula—the unfortunate operation at Anzio in January 1944. As the unhappy U.S. general in command remarked on the eve of that particular landing: 'They will end up by putting me ashore with inadequate forces and get me in a serious jam. Then, who will take the blame?' [7]

Certainly in Korea the J.C.S. had a good case—one of the planning officers for Inchon would remark: 'We drew up a list of every conceivable and natural handicap and Inchon had them all.' Another wrote: 'Make up a list of amphibious don'ts and you have an exact description of the Inchon operation. A lot of us planners felt that if the Inchon operation worked, we'd have to rewrite the textbook.' [8] Eighth Army headquarters in Korea likewise believed an amphibious attack on Inchon to be an unnecessary risk and a grandstand play. Its staff officers naturally preferred that further American reinforcements should go to their own embattled beachhead at Pusan. [9] Nevertheless, with the Pusan defense perimeter uneasily stabilized, by August 23 at an important conference at his headquarters, the disagreement between MacArthur and Collins was essentially settled—on MacArthur's terms.

In an eloquent presentation General MacArthur had expressed the opinion that 'surprise is the most vital element for success in modern war.' Alluding to Gen. James Wolfe's last meeting with his supposedly pessimistic [10] brigadiers before his successful assault on Quebec in 1759, MacArthur reasoned that again it would be precisely the boldness of the Inchon assault which would enable it to succeed—the defenders would not expect such a seemingly foolhardy operation and thus would not take any serious measures against it. As for General Collins's alternative plans of attacking further south, MacArthur said that these would not 'sever . . . the enemy's supply lines or distribution center and would therefore serve little purpose . . . Better no flank movement than such a one. The only result would be a hook-up with Walker's troops on his left. Better send the troops direct to Walker than by such an indirect and costly process.' [11]

MacArthur stressed: 'The amphibious landing is the most powerful tool we have. To employ it properly we must strike hard and deeply into enemy territory.' And in a characteristically dramatic peroration, the General's voice sank and he concluded almost in a whisper: 'We shall land at Inchon and I shall crush them.' [12]

Vice Admiral Joy said after listening to MacArthur's passionate soliloquy: 'My own personal misgivings about Inchon were erased. I believe that the General had persuaded me and all others in the room—with the possible exception of Admiral Sherman—that Inchon could be successful.' Sherman himself would recall that MacArthur was one of the most persuasive men he had ever met and after another private discussion with MacArthur re-

marked: 'I wish I had that man's confidence.' Rear Adm.
James Doyle, who was in charge of the actual landings,
summarized the Navy's general position at this time when
he concluded Inchon was not impossible.[13]

MacArthur had won over his old antagonist, the U.S.
Navy, by declaring that although he himself considered
Inchon a gamble with odds of 5000 to 1, he was accustomed to taking such odds and the Navy had never let
him down. If this last had not been strictly accurate in
the Second World War, it was not a point over which the
Navy would care to cavil, and, in retrospect, Admiral
Sherman would praise MacArthur's grasp of seapower in
the Pacific. MacArthur's argument with Maj. Gen. O. P.
Smith, Commander of the 1st Marine Division, must have
been equally effective. At their first meeting MacArthur
said: 'The landing of the Marines at Inchon will be decisive. It will win the war, and the status of the Marine
Corps will never again be in doubt.' [14]

An analogy from the past, not employed by General
MacArthur on this occasion, testifies to the decisiveness
of a landing at Inchon. In 1894, and again in 1904, the
Japanese had landed at this port, rapidly conquered Korea
as a consequence, and pushed on across the Yalu to seek
a final victory over their enemy in Manchuria. Yet in each
of these limited wars Japan was to feel cheated of a full
victory because of international diplomatic intervention.
At Pearl Harbor in 1941, Japan at last went into an absolute and general war essentially alone—without the understanding or honest support of her allies in the distant
European theater.[15]

Although on August 28 they had given a qualified
approval of his plans for Inchon, as the actual expedition
was getting under way on September 7, the Joint Chiefs

asked MacArthur to estimate again the chances of success. Notwithstanding the fact that all MacArthur's troops in Japan and almost all the ready reserves in the United States were now committed to Korea, General Walker's position at Pusan was still precarious; in the event of a strong enemy reaction there would be no immediate further support available to bail out the Inchon assault force. More optimistically, the Joint Chiefs said that the objective of the Inchon offensive was the destruction of the North Korean Army, a destruction which they expected south of the 38th parallel.

In his reply on the same day, General MacArthur expressed his certitude that Walker would not be overrun. The Far East Commander reiterated that his 'proposed amphibious envelopment was the only hope of wresting the initiative from the enemy, and of creating an opportunity for a decisive blow. Otherwise the United Nations Forces would be involved in a war of attrition of indefinite duration, and of doubtful results, inasmuch as the enemy possessed potentialities of reinforcement far in excess of those available to CINCFE [MacArthur].' [16]

On September 8 the J.C.S. reapproved of the Inchon operation without further mention of alternative landings. The Joint Chiefs also obtained the technically unnecessary approval of President Truman; [17] whatever risks might be taken in the field, the experienced commanders in Washington were guarding against all eventualities.

In the event, as MacArthur's Intelligence had anticipated, the U.S. X Corps encountered almost no naval or air opposition at Inchon on September 15; more surprisingly, there was also very little resistance on the ground. Within a few weeks all of South Korea had been reoccupied, while approximately 135,000 North Koreans

were trapped and taken prisoner by the effect of Mac-
Arthur's dramatic thrust to the enemy's poorly guarded
logistic heart.[18] And, as the General would declare: 'The
star of the [U.S.] Navy and Marine Corps [had] never
shown brighter.' [19]

The U.S. Joint Chiefs were delighted with MacArthur's
success, and the distant British Chiefs of Staff wrote the
American commander: 'We believe that the brilliant conception and masterly execution of the Inchon counter-
stroke which you planned and launched whilst holding
the enemy at bay in the south will rank among the finest
strategic achievements in military history.' [20]

MacArthur's great gamble at Inchon had been vindi-
cated, and confidence in his judgment was becoming
noticeably firmer. But the intoxication ensuing from too
facile and spectacular a success would demand its price.

The Frontiers of Containment

September 15 — October 15, 1950

'In war you know whether you've won or lost; with politicians you think you're winning, but you've lost.' [1]

—Field Marshal Montgomery

'In the world from now on, "neutrality" is only a term for deceiving people.' [2]

—Mao Tse-tung in 1940

'The art of warfare and policy join hands in order to determine together the plan of war in general. Whosoever takes the one or the other alone for his guidance, goes astray. . . . How far, for instance, does a victorious attack lead? Is it permissible to follow it up as far as possible against all enemies? A soldier who is nothing but a soldier, says: Yes; the statesman, however, sees further and knows the limits which policy puts to conquests only too often. The success of arms does not blind him.' [3]

—Friedrich Wilhelm von Zanthier in 1778

'It is extraordinary how rarely it seems to occur to Americans that every victory is a responsibility, and that there are limits on the responsibilities we should invite on ourselves.' [4]

—George F. Kennan

THE DESIRE OF GENERAL MacARTHUR TO cross the 38th parallel had become manifest almost as early as his closely related strategy of landing at Inchon. On July 13, MacArthur had told Generals Collins and Vandenberg: 'I intend to destroy and not to drive back the North Korean forces. I may need to occupy all of North Korea.' [5] A week later, on July 19, President Rhee of Korea cabled Mr. Truman as follows: 'It would be utter folly to attempt to restore the status quo ante, and then await the enemy's pleasure for further attack. . . . For anything less than reunification to come out of these great sacrifices of Koreans and their powerful allies would be unthinkable.' [6] Although in late August General Collins and Admiral Sherman had agreed with MacArthur that anxiety regarding crossing of the 38th parallel need not interfere with his destruction of the North Korean Army, in accepting this position in September, just before Inchon, the National Security Council in Washington recommended that future American decisions should be influenced by the chances of Soviet or Chinese Communist intervention, by the need to consult with America's allies, and by the risk of a general war.

Only on the day of the success of the Inchon landing, September 15, was General MacArthur informed that he might plan operations beyond the 38th parallel, preparatory to crossing it, in the event that neither Russia nor Red China showed signs of entering the war as a consequence. Should major Chinese Communist units cross the 38th parallel, however, MacArthur was told the United States 'would not permit itself to become engaged in a

51

general war' with China, although he might hang on in Korea as long as he had 'a reasonable chance of successful resistance.' [7]

In short, given the success of Inchon, the Truman Administration was already considering going beyond the limits of its own policy of containment, a policy which the Republican party would officially condemn within two years as 'negative, futile and immoral.' [8] Indeed, in late September 1950, Senator William Knowland announced that not to cross the parallel would constitute appeasement of Russia; another Republican Congressman charged the State Department with planning to 'subvert our military victory in Korea' in calling for a United Nations halt at the parallel.[9]

In reality, however, Secretary Acheson had bowed again to the Republican storm and was already engaged in lining up the United Nations to authorize the passage of the parallel. Of his own accord the Secretary of State had given up his previous conviction that the U.N. activities in Korea had been designed 'solely for the purpose of restoring the Republic of Korea to its . . . status prior to the invasion from the North.' [10] The Truman Administration may also have been as eager to profit politically from as impressive a victory as possible before the forthcoming Congressional elections in November 1950, as the Roosevelt Administration had been under similar circumstances in July 1942, when it abandoned its own carefully worked-out conception of over-all strategy in favor of the opportunist landings in North Africa.[11]

On the other hand, the author of the policy of containment, George F. Kennan, held throughout the flush of the Inchon victory that it was a serious mistake not to stabilize the front at the 38th parallel along the narrow waist of central Korea, in the hope of negotiating a settlement with the enemy on that basis.[12] Of course, it is much simpler for the Manichean policy planner to judge the future objectively than for a Secretary of State to act upon such judgments, as Mr. Kennan's subsequent interchanges with Dean Acheson and John Foster Dulles would again reveal.

At first, like Kennan, Foreign Minister Robert Schuman of France was reluctant to transcend the frontiers of containment, but Lester Pearson of Canada supported the United States on this issue.[13] Nevertheless, as Raymond Aron would point out several years later, had the Americans 'voluntarily halted at the old demarcation line they would have been able to claim that they were the victors and been acknowledged as such . . . all over the world.' [14]

On September 27, General MacArthur was told by the Joint Chiefs of Staff that his military objective was now 'the destruction of the North Korean Armed Forces' in North Korea. In executing this mission—still specifically dependent upon there being no indication of a Russian or Red Chinese reaction—MacArthur was warned not to cross the Chinese frontier 'under any circumstances.' As a matter of policy, only South Korean troops should be employed near the Russian or Chinese borders. The U.S. Air Force had already been restricted to tactical targets in North Korea, and the Korean port of Racin, near the important Russian naval base of Vladivostok, could not be bombed.[15]

General MacArthur's plan to carry out his new directive was presented to the J.C.S. without delay on September 28. Assuming the prior destruction of the bulk of the North Korean Army, this plan provided that the main United Nations thrust be made by General Walker's Eighth Army on the left flank toward Pyongyang, the North Korean capital. At the same time a subsidiary amphibious attack by Maj. Gen. Almond's X Corps was to be carried out at Wonsan on the right flank, in the hope of trapping the remnants of the North Korean Army between the two American forces. Non-Korean U.N. troops were to be forbidden to proceed closer than 150 miles to the Chinese or Russian frontiers. Nevertheless, MacArthur saw no indication of any Chinese intention to intervene.[16]

On the same day on which the Joint Chiefs approved of this plan, September 29, the new Secretary of Defense, George Catlett Marshall, told MacArthur: 'We want you to feel unhampered tactically and strategically—to proceed north of the 38th parallel.' The next day MacArthur proposed to Marshall that the United Nations announce to the public the crossing of the now famous parallel. Torn between its desire to exploit more decisively the Inchon landings and its fear of the Communist reactions in Peiping and Moscow, the Truman Administration cautiously ordered MacArthur to play down the significance of a South Korean movement beyond the parallel. Moreover, the United Nations had not yet approved of this decisive step.[17]

As a final gesture toward ending military operations within the frontiers of containment, General MacArthur was permitted to appeal to the Korean Communists on October 1 to surrender unconditionally. The North Korean reaction, however, had already been determined by the Chinese Communist decision on or before September 30 to the effect that 'Communist China would not stand aside' if North Korea were invaded.[18] Like the Russian government in 1904,[19] Peiping was about to make the crossing of the 38th parallel by her enemy a *casus belli*.

On October 3 the Chinese Communist Foreign Minister informed the sympathetic Indian Ambassador at Peiping,

K. M. Pannikar, that the Red Chinese would intervene in the event that U.N. forces, as opposed to merely South Korean troops, crossed the 38th parallel.[20] The Administration immediately relayed this information to General MacArthur, although Washington remained in some doubt of how much the Chinese Communists were bluffing on this issue.[21] The Administration did know, however, that large numbers of Red Chinese troops were moving hurriedly toward Manchuria, and in Korea, at least, both the U.S. Eighth Army Commander, General Walker, and the South Korean Defense Minister evidently took the Chinese Communist threat seriously enough to have advocated halting the advance of the U.N. troops.[22] But the South Korean Defense Minister's superior, President Syngman Rhee, had already declared: 'Where is the 38th parallel? . . . . It is non-existent. I am going all the way to the Yalu, and the United Nations can't stop me.'[23]

Notwithstanding specific warnings from the Indian delegate to the United Nations, Sir Benegal Rau, that such action might result in the extension or prolongation of the Korean War, on October 7 the British delegate, Mr. Kenneth Younger, introduced a resolution in the U.N. General Assembly authorizing United Nations operations north of the 38th parallel. With an enthusiasm which must have gratified Syngman Rhee and his Republican allies in the U.S. Senate far more than his own Labour party, Ernest Bevin, the British Foreign Minister, then in New York, declared that in the future there could be 'no South Koreans, no North Koreans; just Koreans.' Confronted with this briefly aggressive British attitude the General Assembly passed Mr. Younger's resolution.[24] The principal American ally had not restrained Washington at the decisive moment.

Nevertheless, not surprisingly, on October 9 with the approval of President Truman the Joint Chiefs sent Mac-Arthur an amplification of his entire directive regarding the possibility of Chinese Communist intervention. This read: 'Hereafter in the event of the open or covert employment anywhere in Korea of major Chinese Communist units, without prior announcement, you should continue . . . as long as, in your judgment, action by forces now under your control offers a reasonable chance of success. In any case you will obtain authorization from Washington prior to taking any military action against objectives in Chinese territory.' Privately the President had resolved to still any doubts regarding the settlement of the Korean problem by means of a personal interview with General MacArthur.[25]

The Administration's incertitude was hardly resolved when on the next day, October 10, the Peiping radio asserted that the General Assembly resolution authorizing the crossing of the 38th parallel was illegal and was opposed by the majority of the world's population. The Red Chinese broadcast repeated its earlier conclusion: 'We cannot stand idly by. . . . The Chinese people love peace, but in order to defend peace, they never will be afraid to oppose aggressive war.'[26] Whether aggressive or not, in transcending a policy of containment the Truman Administration had unmistakably gone beyond the terms of defensive warfare, although its hesitations regarding its new course were not yet seen as based on fundamental realities of power and public opinion.

Since President Truman felt there was no substitute for personal conversation with the commander in the field, Secretary of Defense Marshall, in recommending to Mac-Arthur that he become reacquainted with the United

States, asked MacArthur whether he preferred to meet the President in Hawaii or Wake Island in the Pacific.[27] Supposedly grudging his trip to meet President Truman as much as the one he had made in 1944 to see President Roosevelt, MacArthur was unwilling to unbend any more than he could help; he chose Wake Island and made the politically weaker President travel further to see him. But MacArthur undoubtedly hoped that he could charm Mr. Truman as successfully as he had Franklin Roosevelt. After Roosevelt's somewhat unexpected sympathy with his arguments for seizing Luzon rather than Formosa, MacArthur is alleged to have remarked: 'You know the President is a man of great vision, once things are explained to him.' [28]

Certainly the meeting at Wake went smoothly enough, and with good fortune in future military operations outwardly tolerable relations between the President and the General might have been preserved. In fact, the relations between the two principals at Wake may have become friendly enough for MacArthur to have told Mr. Truman with some bitterness that he had let the Republicans embarrass him with presidential possibilities in 1948 and that he did not intend to repeat the experience.[29]

The Wake Conference commenced on October 15 with a statement by General MacArthur that he believed all enemy resistance would end throughout Korea by Thanksgiving. By Christmas, MacArthur hoped to withdraw the Eighth Army to Japan, leaving two American divisions behind until elections were held in Korea in January. Then the remaining troops were to be withdrawn because, as MacArthur put it, 'all occupations are failures.' The President agreed with this democratic sentiment and General Bradley was equally pleased to hear that a first-class

American division in Korea would shortly be freed for service in Europe.[30]

After going out of his way to assure his superiors that 'no commander in the history of war has ever had more complete and adequate support from all agencies in Washington' [31] than himself, General MacArthur was asked by the President for his opinion of the chances for Chinese or Soviet intervention. In a reply which could never be forgotten nor be effaced from the Administration's records MacArthur said: 'Very little. Had they [the Chinese Communists] interfered in the first or second months [of the Korean War] it would have been decisive. We are no longer fearful of their intervention. We no longer stand hat in hand. The Chinese have 300,000 men in Manchuria. Of these probably not more than 100-125,000 are distributed along the Yalu River. Only 50-60,000 could be gotten across the Yalu River. They have no Air Force. Now that we have bases for our Air Force in Korea, if the Chinese tried to get down to Pyongyang there would be the greatest slaughter.' [32]

MacArthur did not believe that the Russians either could put ground troops into Korea in the winter or that their 'fairly good' air force in Siberia could co-operate effectively with Chinese Communist ground troops in the American fashion.[33] In this connection, the General remarked: 'I believe Russian air would bomb the Chinese as often as they would bomb us.' [34] Mis-estimation of enemy capabilities had been a MacArthur tendency from the old days in the Philippines and, indeed, may have contributed to the departure from Manila of his former aide, Maj. Dwight D. Eisenhower.[35]

That MacArthur's anticipations of the future were profoundly misconceived was, however, not yet apparent, and it is not to be wondered at that President Truman thought his conference with the General had been very satisfactory. One of the principal participants at the meeting, Gen. Omar Bradley, believed that Mr. Truman and General MacArthur had reached agreement, even on the problem of Formosa, in a private conversation during the meeting; moreover, evidently neither Bradley nor others present called into question MacArthur's estimates of the future—all assumed that a final victory was in the bag in the customary American tradition.[36]

On behalf of both MacArthur's optimism and of the over-confidence of the Administration, it must be noted that on October 12 the Central Intelligence Agency reported to the President that, although the Chinese Communists had the capability of effective intervention, such intervention would not necessarily be decisive. C.I.A. had then seen no convincing indication of any Chinese intention to resort to a full-scale entry into the Korean War. The C.I.A. had finally concluded that the Chinese Communists feared the consequences of war with the United States and that their intervention was thus 'not probable in 1950.'[37] It is, of course, perfectly possible that U.S. intelligence agencies had underestimated the capabilities of the Chinese Communists as much as their intentions. In any event, whether justifiable or not as an intelligence procedure, involving, as it had in 1941 and may have again in 1960,[38] the convenient postulate that the enemy would act in accord with an American conception of the rational, in November 1950 it was essentially the Chinese Communists' intentions which the United States was trying to evaluate.

Apart from these general American misconceptions there is little doubt that by the time of the Wake Conference the United States, having made a great effort to rescue South Korea, could not just stop there—American opinion needed the further compensation of some form of victory for its enormous effort in Korea, and the cautious and realistic policy of containment was one of the first victims of this overwhelming psychic need.

VI

Dizziness from Success

October 16 — November 28, 1950

'A good soldier, whether he leads a platoon or an army, is expected to look backward as well as forward, but he must think only forward.' [1]

—Douglas MacArthur, in 1933

'. . . in order to draw an enemy into a fight unfavorable to him but favorable to us, we should often engage him when he is on the move and should look for such conditions favorable to ourselves in the advantageousness of the terrain . . . and fatigue and inadvertence on the part of the enemy. This means that we should allow the enemy . . . "to penetrate deep." ' [2]

—Mao Tse-tung

'The office of the statesman is to determine and to indicate to the military authorities the national interests most vital to be defended, as well as the objects of conquest or destruction most injurious to the enemy in view of the political exigencies which the military power only subserves.' [3]

—Admiral Mahan

'I can't tell you how disgusted I am becoming with these wretched politicians.' [4]

—Gen. George McClellan, October 1861

AN INTER-SERVICE DISAGREEMENT GREETED General MacArthur on his return from the brief encounter at Wake. Anticipating trapping the enemy again as at Inchon, the Commander of the U.S. X Corps, Gen. Edward Almond, preferred to have the U.S. Navy ferry his corps forward by sea—on this occasion to the Korean northeast coast port of Wonsan. In the process Almond could convey his heavy matériel by ship far more easily than on the battered and inadequate Korean land routes. Short of amphibious and support shipping, and already suspicious of the great mine barrage awaiting them at Wonsan, the U.S. Navy believed that the American Army could go overland as rapidly as the lightly equipped South Koreans.[5]

MacArthur chose Almond's view primarily, it would seem, because of the limited capacity of Inchon as a port and because of his faith in amphibious operations per se. Thus the amphibious landing at Wonsan was finally staged in late October, eleven days after the city had been occupied by South Korean troops marching on foot. But the most serious consequence of MacArthur's decision to favor Almond was to accentuate the separation, both in command and in supply, of the former's X Corps from General Walker's Eighth Army.

General Walker and MacArthur's own staff planners opposed this violation of standard U.S. Army command organization. Moreover, moving most of Almond's corps out of Inchon again by sea would close down this vital port to all incoming supplies for a full three weeks, thus actually delaying rather than expediting the advance of the Eighth

Army. Although the Joint Chiefs of Staff would suggest, if not order, a unification of Walker's and Almond's forces under Walker's command, this was not done by General MacArthur. Throughout the period following his recall, MacArthur would deny that the two American units in North Korea lacked operational co-ordination. He maintained that they were naturally separated by the mountains of North Korea and that his headquarters in Tokyo offered sufficient unity for all tactical purposes.[6]

MacArthur's desire to keep a closer grip tactically on his subordinates, perhaps as a consequence of a distrust of Walker's capacity, perhaps as a result of his closeness to Almond, may also have influenced the Far East Commander. Finally, the personal antipathy between Almond and Walker, which was so characteristic of MacArthur's staffs as a whole, provided another intangible factor.[7]

On another potentially important point a discrepancy between MacArthur's position and that of the Joint Chiefs was appearing. On his own initiative, on October 24 MacArthur advised his field commanders that United Nations troops other than South Koreans could now occupy any part of North Korean territory. MacArthur justified this order on the grounds that there no longer appeared to be any prospect of an enemy surrender. He enjoined Walker and Almond to 'drive forward with all speed and with full utilization of all their force.'[8] Somewhat inconsistently, MacArthur's intelligence chief, General Willoughby, described the North Koreans as 'a rabble in arms' of some 25,000 men pursued by over 200,000 United Nations soldiers.[9]

The same day the Joint Chiefs informed MacArthur that his new directive was 'not in consonance' with their earlier 'instructions' to the effect that only South Korean troops might approach the Chinese or Russian frontiers. Going further than he had over the issue of the divided command in North Korea, the U.S. Army Chief of Staff, Gen. J. Lawton Collins, would eventually criticize MacArthur for not obtaining clearance from the J.C.S. on this directive. Nevertheless, when MacArthur replied to the Joint Chiefs on October 25, explaining that it was a 'military necessity' to employ his total strength near the frontier since the South Koreans alone were dangerously weak, the Joint Chiefs accepted MacArthur's explanation without ordering any changes. Perhaps they were lulled by the General's assurances at the same time that he 'would take all precautions,' [10] although his further explanation that he possessed authority from the Secretary of Defense to modify his instructions along this line may not have particularly pleased the J.C.S. It will be recalled that on September 29 Marshall had told MacArthur 'to feel unhampered tactically and strategically' in the course of destroying the North Korean forces.[11]

For the press and among intimates in this period, however, MacArthur was extremely optimistic, declaring publicly: 'The war is very definitely coming to an end shortly. With the closing of that trap there should be an end to organized resistance.' MacArthur was currently planning for a permanent occupation force in Korea of only one American division.[12]

His perennial antagonist, the U.S. State Department, was now more pessimistic about the chances of Chinese intervention, which, after October 19, it no longer was inclined to dismiss as a bluff. In accord with this newly accentuated anxiety, on October 21 the Joint Chiefs asked MacArthur not to bomb a power plant on the Chinese-Korean frontier near Sinuiju which supplied electricity to

Manchuria as well as North Korea. On the other hand, having run out of targets in Korea short of the Russian or Chinese frontiers, like MacArthur, the U.S. Air Force in the Far East was preparing to go home in the near future.[13]

Whatever the hopes of the American Commanders in Japan and Korea, the State Department fears were justified. Between October 24 and 28, South Korean troops near the Yalu were attacked by forces at last positively identified as Chinese. Interrogation of enemy prisoners revealed that the three or more Chinese Communist divisions involved had crossed the Korean frontier on October 16, one day after the meeting at Wake Island.[14] Although General Willoughby would declare at the end of October, 'From a tactical viewpoint, with victorious American divisions in full deployment, it would appear that the auspicious time for intervention [by the Chinese] has long since passed,' MacArthur's Intelligence nonetheless doubled or tripled early October estimates of the size of the Chinese Red forces along the Yalu.[15]

On a night in late October, two battalions of the U.S. 1st Cavalry Division were attacked and badly battered by Red Chinese. Like MacArthur, this American division did not know whether the action of these Chinese troops represented any official policy of the Chinese Communist Government. On November 3, the U.S. 24th Division hurriedly retreated some fifty miles to avoid a new Chinese threat to its supply lines. In Tokyo General MacArthur expressed surprise and asked why; in Washington, General Bradley jumped to the opposite conclusion that 'only diplomacy could save [General] Walker's right flank,'[16] On the Korean east coast, the U.S. X Corps Commander, Gen. Edward Almond, remained quite optimistic, but his subordinates in the 1st Marine Division hereafter anticipated a serious intervention by the Chinese Communists and made their preparations accordingly.[17]

Although on November 5 a prominent Chinese Communist journal had asserted that the United States was a 'paper tiger' which 'can be fully defeated,'[18] the Central Intelligence Agency, U.S. Army G-2 in Washington and MacArthur's Intelligence were all inclined to accept Chinese Communist assertions that in establishing a purported 'cordon sanitaire' along the frontier their so-called 'volunteer' troops had entered Korea only for the sake of protecting Manchuria and the Yalu power plants. The U.S. Joint Chiefs consequently found themselves most uncertain regarding their future course of action, particularly because they had not considered the possibility of a limited intervention by the Chinese before it appeared. Yet, if the war was persisting in not responding to American military preconceptions of its nature, the J.C.S. made no attempt to control the movements of MacArthur's command more tightly; equally uncertain of the future, the State Department preferred to consider the issue a military affair.[19]

Although, in response to a request from the J.C.S. on November 4, he still maintained that an all-out Chinese Communist intervention constituted their least likely course of action, MacArthur had already concluded that the problem of a Chinese entry had been removed 'from the realm of the academic' into 'a serious proximate threat.' To the Joint Chiefs, however, the General stressed that so far the evidence was insufficient for any final conclusions.[20]

In a special communiqué on November 6, remarkably anticipating what he would say at the end of the month, MacArthur announced that he had evaded a 'possible trap'

which had been 'surreptitiously laid' by the Chinese Communists. But he now faced a 'new and fresh army' which
was supported by large reserves 'beyond the limits of
our present sphere of military action.' [21] At the same time
MacArthur ordered the Far East Air Force to bomb the
principal bridge which supplied the Chinese in North
Korea from across their Yalu River frontier.

When Washington heard of this last order some hours
before its execution, the State Department urgently re-
minded the President of an agreement with the British
not to bomb Manchurian targets without prior consultation with London. The Joint Chiefs then ordered Mac-
Arthur to postpone all bombing of targets within five
miles of the Manchurian border until further notice.[22]

MacArthur's instant reply to this limitation on his action
was vigorous, and to some extent successful, since as a
result he was allowed to bomb the Korean end of the Yalu
bridges.[23] In effect appealing above the Joint Chiefs to
the President himself, MacArthur wrote:

> Men and matériel in large force are pouring across all
> bridges over the Yalu from Manchuria. This movement not
> only jeopardizes but threatens the ultimate destruction of
> the forces under my command. The actual movement across
> the river can be accomplished under cover of darkness and the
> distance between the river and our lines is so short that the
> forces can be deployed against our troops without being
> seriously subjected to air interdiction. The only way to stop
> this reinforcement of the enemy is the destruction of these
> bridges and the subjection of all installations in the north
> area supporting the enemy advance to the maximum of our
> air destruction. Every hour that this is postponed will be
> paid for dearly in American and other United Nations blood.
> The main crossing at Sinuiju was to be hit within the next
> few hours and the mission is actually being mounted. Under

the gravest protest that I can make, I am suspending this strike and carrying out your instructions. What I had ordered is entirely within the scope of the rules of war and the resolutions and directions which I have received from the United Nations, and constitutes no slightest act of belligerency against Chinese territory, in spite of the outrageous international lawlessness emanating therefrom. I cannot over-emphasize the disastrous effect, both physical and psychological, that will result from the restrictions which you are imposing. I trust that the matter be immediately brought to the attention of the President as I believe your instructions may well result in a calamity of major proportion for which I cannot accept the responsibility without his personal and direct understanding of the situation. Time is so essential that I request immediate reconsideration of your decision pending which complete compliance will of course be given to your order.[24]

Perhaps emboldened by the comparative success of his letter of November 6, the next day MacArthur went further in two messages to the Joint Chiefs. First, although conceding that he might be forced to retreat should the Chinese be again reinforced, MacArthur proposed a new American advance to take an 'accurate measure . . . of the enemy strength.' [25]

His U.S. Eighth Army Commander, Gen. Walton Walker, also opposed any immediate retreat to the short defensive line of Sinuiju-Wonsan in North Korea. But in opposition to MacArthur, Walker disapproved of a risky and rapid advance on the Yalu for the sake of keeping the Eighth Army, in the ambiguous words of MacArthur's own staff, 'free to maneuver.' [26]

In his second message on November 7, he requested the right of hot pursuit for his fighter planes actually engaged in combat with the enemy over the Yalu frontier, so that they could reply to attacks by Russian MIGs recently aimed at them from under the cover of neutral Chinese territory. The Far East Commander wrote: 'The effect of this abnormal condition upon the morale and combat efficiency of both air and ground troops is major. Unless corrective measures are promptly taken this factor can assume decisive proportions.' [27]

Although the President, the Joint Chiefs, and the State Department approved of this request, several United Nations powers involved in Korea protested so strongly that the idea of hot pursuit was eventually dropped. The State Department was unable to convince a single ally of those consulted that such action would be consistent with the official American aim of doing 'everything possible to localize [the] conflict in Korea.' In mid-November, it might be noted, the Allied Powers had become particularly disturbed by a secret report from Peiping that the Russians were threatening aerial retaliation if the United Nations bombed Manchurian fields. [28]

The intelligence agencies of Australia, Sweden, Burma, and the Netherlands had all now decided that the Chinese Communists were not bluffing on their threats to enter the war; nevertheless, in Washington the Central Intelligence Agency still concluded that for the immediate future Chinese Communist operations in Korea would probably continue to be defensive in nature. In addition C.I.A. believed that while the Russians might not be willing to go to war in the Far East themselves, they would be delighted to gain a freer hand in Europe as a result of a deeper American involvement in Asia. Dissatisfied with the comparative blandness of these conclusions, President Truman ordered that a special effort be made to determine the intentions of the Chinese Communists. [29]

Secretary of Defense Marshall considered it desirable to assuage General MacArthur's disappointment on this occasion without, however, much apparent effect. Violating his own long-held principle of not sending personal letters to officers in the field, Marshall wrote:

The discussions and decisions here are heavily weighted with the extremely delicate situation we have before the Security Council of the United Nations whose meeting tomorrow may have fateful consequences. We all realize your difficulty in fighting a desperate battle in a mountainous region under winter conditions and with a multinational force in all degrees of preparedness. I also understand, I think, the difficulty involved in conducting such a battle under necessarily limiting conditions and the necessity of keeping the distant headquarters closely informed of developments and decisions. However, this appears to be unavoidable, but I want you to know that I understand your problems. Everyone here, Defense, State and the President, is intensely desirous of supporting you in the most effective manner within our means. At the same time we are faced with an extremely grave international problem which could so easily lead into a world disaster.

To his explanation Marshall also added an inquiry:

Incidentally, for my own personal information, do you feel that the hydroelectric and reservoir situation is probably the dominant consideration in this apparently last minute move by the Chinese Communists, incited by the Soviets to protect their war interests in the Far East? [30]

MacArthur's reply played down the significance of the hydroelectric system as a major factor in Communist decisions. During a somewhat inaccurate discussion of recent Chinese history the General emphasized instead what he believed to be 'the aggressive belligerency of the Chinese Communists.' [31] In a fundamental disagreement with the Administration on underlying assumptions, MacArthur felt that the Chinese Communist activities in Korea had always been aggressive, not defensive, in motive. Presumably for this reason he criticized the current State Department, British, Canadian, and French efforts to create a disarmed buffer zone along the Yalu River frontier as a form of appeasement on the lines of the Munich Conference in 1938. In defense of his policy of advancing to the Yalu, MacArthur concluded: 'To give up any portion of North Korea to the aggression of the Chinese Communists would be the greatest defeat of the free world in modern times.' [32]

MacArthur's policy here—for policy this explicitly was —did not answer the strictly military objection of the British at this time that he lacked the resources to achieve and to hold the Yalu line without recourse to bombing the Chinese Communist bases in Manchuria. But, as the U.S. Army Director of G-3, Maj. Gen. Charles Bolte, told General Collins, it was easier to support MacArthur, since in any case he would not change his mind. The State and Defense Departments then prepared a compromise proposal by which MacArthur would advance only to the approaches of the Yalu and halt on the 128th meridian on the Korean northeast coast. [33]

As a consequence of MacArthur's attitude, the Joint Chiefs recommended that the problem of Chinese Communist intervention should be settled, if possible, by political means, that MacArthur's directives should not be changed, and that the United States should prepare to face the increased danger of a general war. In a meeting of the National Security Council on November 9 to consider these recommendations, General Bradley discussed in some detail the question of Chinese Communist intentions. Bradley believed that the United States could hold its present positions in North Korea, although he was less optimistic than MacArthur had been regarding the effect of bombing the Yalu bridges. In this connection Gen. Bedell Smith of C.I.A. observed that the Yalu would soon be frozen over in any event. Bradley also recognized that a line further back than the present one would be more defensible militarily, whatever its political implications. One of the frustrating circumstances for either side in the Korean struggle was that, while an advance increased the area of political control, it weakened each army logistically through extending its own and shortening the enemy supply lines. This basic fact of logistics, as much as piecemeal reinforcements,[34] exerted a strong and constant pressure for a stalemate near the center of the narrow and rugged peninsula.

General Bradley was uncertain as to how much pressure the United States could resist in Korea without having recourse to the bombing of enemy bases in Manchuria, but the Joint Chiefs agreed that only the United Nations could make a decision on attacking these bases. Toward the end of the discussion Secretary Marshall reflected the usual uneasiness regarding the wide dispersion of General Almond's troops on the Korean east coast. Secretary of State Acheson then summarized the National Security Council's essential agreement with the Joint Chiefs' conclusions on policy.[35] Short of an unmistakable defeat, neither the Administration nor the Joint Chiefs were going to curb MacArthur's program effectively so long as it remained within the confines of Korea.[36]

In accordance with these conclusions, and in a particular effort to reassure both the Chinese Communist Government and the United States European Allies regarding American intentions, on November 16 President Truman publicly declared:

> Speaking for the United States Government and people, I can give assurance that we are supporting and are acting within the limits of United Nations policy in Korea, and that we have never at any time entertained any intention to carry hostilities into China; so far as the United States is concerned, I wish to state unequivocally that because of our deep devotion to the cause of world peace, and our long-standing friendship for the people of China, we will take every honorable step to prevent any extension of the hostilities in the Far East.
>
> If the Chinese authorities or people believe otherwise, it can only be because they are being deceived by those whose advantage it is to prolong and extend hostilities in the Far East against the interest of all Far Eastern people.[37]

Within a week the British Government had followed the President's assurances with a promise to Peiping that the U.N. forces had no designs on Chinese territory or interests. The American command in the Far East notwithstanding, the United Nations governments involved in Korea were leaving the Communist Government as little cause for intervention as possible. Indeed, as early at November 10, the U.N. Security Council itself had invited the Chinese Communists to send a representative to New York to explain their position.[38] It is, of course, difficult to determine if Peiping took seriously these diplomatic reassurances or whether the aggressive manner of General MacArthur influenced it more in its final decision to enter the Korean War,[39] since to the extent that Communist evidence on this issue is available it is apt to be false.

On November 24, in a special communiqué to the United Nations, General MacArthur proclaimed that his final drive to end the war was 'now approaching its decisive effort.' In language which he must soon have regretted and which could not have proved palatable to Peiping, his communiqué read:

> The gigantic U.N. pincers moved according to schedule today.—The air forces, in full strength, completely interdicted the rear areas and an air reconnaissance beyond the enemy line, and along the entire length of the Yalu River border, showed little sign of hostile military activity. The left wing of envelopment advanced against stubborn and failing resistance. The right wing, gallantly supported by naval, air and surface action, continued to exploit its commanding position.
>
> Our losses were extraordinarily light. The logistic situation is fully geared to sustain offensive operations. The justice of our cause and promise of early completion of our mission is reflected in the morale of troops and commanders alike.[40]

During the Second World War the tendency of MacArthur's headquarters to announce victory prematurely was so well recognized that the U.S. Navy had circulated far and wide a savage little jingle on the matter.[41] But during what the U.S. Marine Corps historians have termed the 'end-of-the-war atmosphere' prevailing at MacArthur's headquarters during most of November 1950, such pronouncements must have seemed natural.[42]

In a private explanation to the Joint Chiefs on the commencement of his offensive, MacArthur said: 'Had they [the Chinese Communists] entered at the time we were beleaguered behind our Pusan perimeter beachhead, the hazard would have been far more grave than it is now that we hold the initiative.'[43] Here MacArthur characteristically missed the political point that during the period

75

of North Korean victory the Chinese Communists had no incentive to enter the Korean War—it was only his victory at Inchon and its exploitation thereafter which had spurred the Chinese Communists to take the plunge. But it is probably unreasonable to expect many soldiers to see the potential liaison between a military victory and a political defeat—even with the lessons of 1945 so freshly in mind.

In subsequent explanations of his decision at this time to launch a general offensive up to the actual frontiers of China, General MacArthur has said that a 'reconnaissance in force' was the only method available 'to find out what the enemy had and what his intentions were,' and that such a reconnaissance constituted 'the final test of Chinese intentions.' [44]

During the Senate Hearings in 1951, General Collins would question this explanation of MacArthur's, saying that the Far East commander was 'bent upon the destruction of the North Korean forces.' Collins also asserted that it was perfectly possible to halt before reaching the Yalu.[45] And a U.S. Army historian, Louis Morton, has observed caustically: 'A reconnaissance in force which leaves the commander with practically no reserves is a somewhat unusual maneuver,' while the defeat which resulted was 'certainly an expensive way to discover the enemy's intentions.' [46] It may well be that MacArthur feared what he conceived to be failure in Korea more than he feared the Chinese.[47]

MacArthur's intelligence chief, Maj. Gen. Charles Willoughby, for one, is willing to grant that MacArthur's supposed spoiling attack evoked a premature move on the part of the Chinese Communists and thus upset what Willoughby has considered the Chinese timetable to trap the United Nations forces.[48] Like MacArthur, today Willoughby would appear to have assumed the all-out entry of the Chinese Communists before it actually appeared, although at the time small enough preparations seem to have been made to cope with such a result. Another MacArthur aide, Maj. Gen. Courtney Whitney, has justified MacArthur's final offensive on the astonishing grounds that it was 'one of the most successful military maneuvers in modern history.' [49] And MacArthur himself, in language only slightly better calculated to avoid ridicule, has said: 'The disposition of those [United Nations] troops, in my opinion, could not have been improved upon had I known the Chinese were going to attack.' [50]

After mountainous testimony General MacArthur evidently came to recognize that this position was as untenable in debate as it had proved in the field. In his letter to Senator Byrd in 1953, he offered a more up-to-date explanation of his advance to the Yalu, namely that (notwithstanding the J.C.S. and British advance warning on precisely this issue) he had counted upon the bombing of the Chinese supply lines in Manchuria in the event of the last-minute Chinese Communist intervention.[51] By 1956 Generals MacArthur and Whitney had concluded that, among the many leaks of the Korean War, the Chinese Communists had been informed by the British diplomatic deserters to Communism, Guy Burgess and Donald MacLean, that they need have no fear of an American aerial counterattack against Manchuria if they entered the Korean War.[52] Since after Alger Hiss it was improbable that anyone would attempt to defend Burgess and MacLean, they could scarcely be improved upon as ideal scapegoats for a largely unnecessary defeat.

On the much discussed question of the intelligence

warnings concerning the probable Chinese Communist response to MacArthur's offensive, there is decidedly less agreement, even in MacArthur's own camp. General Whitney has blamed the Central Intelligence Agency for its delayed report to MacArthur on November 24 to the effect that 'there is no evidence that the Chinese Communists plan major offensive operations in Korea.'[53] General Willoughby has declared that this C.I.A. report did not reach Tokyo until after November 28, and therefore has blamed C.I.A. for still greater tardiness, although clearly in this interpretation the much abused intelligence agency cannot simultaneously be charged with having lulled MacArthur's fears before the major Red Chinese attack on November 25-28.[54]

Gen. Bedell Smith, then the C.I.A. chief, has complained of the attitude of General Willoughby in assisting him on intelligence matters, an important issue since a large share of American intelligence in the Far East came from Willoughby's own sources.[55] Since Willoughby's estimates of the number of Chinese Communists in Korea in mid-November varied from 25,000 to 76,000, all supposedly in poor shape (when there were actually some 300,000 well-trained Chinese already across the Yalu), Bedell Smith's feelings can be understood.[56] General MacArthur himself had no complaint whatsoever that the C.I.A. had let him down—a position, for once, very similar to that of President Truman.[57] At least, notwithstanding MacArthur's denial, Admiral Sherman's statement that Chinese Communist intervention was seriously considered by the Administration appears valid, although Secretary Acheson has admitted that on November 24 Washington still expected only a gradual increase in Red Chinese activities in Korea. Sherman, who was frequently in agreement with

MacArthur, has testified that he 'had worried about it [a Chinese Communist intervention] for a long while' and that he had received plenty of warnings to whet such fears.[58]

The last of these warnings was given to MacArthur on November 24, the day on which he announced his final offensive. In what General Collins has cited as a specific violation of his instructions, in this offensive MacArthur had again ordered all of his troops to march directly to the frontier without so informing the Joint Chiefs. When advised again by the J.C.S. to keep his non-South Korean troops away from the immediate vicinity of the Yalu in order not to provoke the Chinese Communists unnecessarily, MacArthur replied that military necessity compelled him to send all of his forces to the border, but that he planned to withdraw his American troops to Japan as soon as possible. On MacArthur's behalf it must be noted that, as in October, on this occasion the J.C.S. did not give him positive orders to pull back his non-Korean personnel; in retrospect General Bradley has said that, while he would have disposed of the troops differently himself, he never interfered with the tactics of subordinate commanders.[59] This was standard U.S. Army practice.

Within a day or two of the opening of the final American offensive, during November 25-28, the Chinese Communists struck in force. From south of the Yalu River, where a Chinese army arose undetected and drove through the South Korean II Corps deep into the U.S. 2nd Division, to 150 miles away, above the Korean east coast, where the U.S. 1st Marine Division would shortly find itself cut off from the sea, the Chinese Communists were in action.[60] General MacArthur's casually reassuring remark of a few days before to some American front-line troops that they

79

would be home for Christmas dinner would now embarrass the Truman Administration's efforts to uphold his
prestige as much as it would serve to humiliate the General
himself.[61]

General MacArthur's special communiqué to the United
Nations on November 28 said:

> Enemy reactions developed in the course of our assault
> operations of the past four days disclose that a major segment
> of the Chinese continental forces in army, corps and divisional
> organization of an aggregate strength of over 200,000 men
> is now arrayed against the United Nations forces in North
> Korea. . . . Consequently, we face an entirely new war.[62]

As Secretary Acheson would point out in his testimony
in the Senate hearing, MacArthur's estimate of Chinese
Communist intentions and capabilities had 'turned out to
be wrong.' And, as Senator Saltonstall put it, in a larger but
less flattering context to the Administration: 'They [the
Chinese Communists] really fooled us when it comes right
down to it; didn't they?' Secretary of State Acheson could
only reply: 'Yes, sir.' [63]

VII

An Entirely New War

November 28, 1950 — January 17, 1951

'Enemy Advances, We Retreat; Enemy Halts, We Harass; Enemy Tires, We Attack; Enemy Retreats, We Pursue.' [1]

—Mao Tse-tung

'They have outnumbered us everywhere, but we have not lost our honor. This army has acted magnificently. I thank my friends in Washington for our repulse.' [2]

—Gen. George McClellan, June 27, 1862

'I like commanders on land and sea and in the air to feel that between them and all forms of public criticism the Government stands like a strong bulkhead. They ought to have a fair chance, and more than one chance. Men may make mistakes and learn from their mistakes. Men may have bad luck, and their luck may change. But anyhow you will not get generals to run risks unless they feel they have behind them a strong government.' [3]

—Winston Churchill, July 2, 1942

'I have so often in my life been mistaken that I no longer blush for it.' [4]

—Napoleon

THE FIRST REACTIONS IN WASHINGTON TO the gamble which had failed were reflected in a meeting of the National Security Council on November 28. The Council was confronted with MacArthur's simultaneous orders to bomb the Yalu bridges as well as the General's request for basic new decisions on the part of the United Nations, since in his own words his command was 'now faced with conditions beyond its control or strength.' [5]

In disagreement with Maj. Gen. Emmett O'Donnell, Chief of the Far East Air Force Bomber Command, General Bradley and the Joint Chiefs of Staff were reluctant to authorize the American bombing of points in Manchuria on the somewhat debatable grounds that the then still weak Chinese Communist Air Force could damage the crowded American airfields in Korea and Japan more than the U.S. Air Force could hurt the enemy bases in Manchuria. Secretary of Defense Marshall supported the Joint Chiefs on another point—the necessity for avoiding a general war with China which, among other things, would halt any build-up of American military strength in Europe. Secretary of State Acheson chimed in with the opinion that, if the United States successfully attacked the Manchurian airfields, Russia would 'cheerfully' enter the war, a hypothesis already essential to President Truman's way of thinking. And Averell Harriman said that to maintain its leadership of the free world the United States must assure the immediate appointment of a supreme commander for NATO. [6] Obviously the Democratic Administration's interest still remained in Europe, whatever might be happening along the Yalu.

The next day, November 29, General MacArthur cabled to ask for 50-60,000 Chinese Nationalist troops from Formosa as reinforcements. As General Collins put it, the U.S. Regular Army had already been 'skinned down . . . to [the] bone' for Korea, and there were no more American combat troops left in Japan. MacArthur also pointed out that in his opinion the earlier arguments against provoking the Red Chinese were now no longer valid, whereas his need for manpower was urgent. In their reply on the same day the Joint Chiefs stressed both the inadequate training of the Chinese Nationalists according to MacArthur's own survey party in September, and the rather improbable threat of a Chinese Communist invasion of Formosa.[7]

After further consultations with the State Department the J.C.S. concluded in their message to MacArthur as follows:

> Your proposal is being considered. It involves world-wide consequences. We shall have to consider the possibility that it would disrupt the united position of the nations associated with us in the United Nations, and have us isolated. It may be wholly unacceptable to the commonwealth countries to have their forces employed with Nationalist Chinese. It might extend hostilities to Formosa and other areas. Incidentally, our position of leadership in the Far East is being most seriously compromised in the United Nations. The utmost care will be necessary to avoid the disruption of the essential Allied line-up in that organization.[8]

United States Government policy was noticeably less acquiescent to MacArthur in defeat than it had been during the General's brief honeymoon with victory.

The mood of mounting anxiety in Washington which had resulted in these cautious reactions found parallels in the Far East. Despite MacArthur's subsequent insistence that the American troops in Korea were not 'badly defeated,' but were merely engaged in a withdrawal 'planned ... from the beginning' in the event of a major Chinese Communist assault,[9] on November 28 the U.S. Navy Commander in the Far East began to prepare for a possible evacuation of American forces in North Korea by sea. On November 29-30 the Chief of Naval Operations in Washington, Adm. Forrest Sherman, authorized his subordinates in the Far East to retain both an aircraft carrier and empty cargo ships due for departure from Japanese or Korean waters. General incertitude regarding the future and the particular possibility of Russian intervention were factors in Sherman's decision.[10] Moreover, amphibious evacuations were not unflattering to the Navy, at least.

On November 29 the Joint Chiefs as a whole approved of MacArthur's plans to go on the defensive, and by December 9 General Almond's X Corps had received MacArthur's directive to prepare to evacuate his troops by sea. Despite his annoyance, MacArthur was also ordered by the J.C.S. to co-ordinate Almond's retreat with General Walker's Eighth Army, so as to diminish the chances of a much-feared enemy movement between the two widely separated American units.[11] Since General MacArthur could no longer expect reinforcements from the United States, he explained to Walker and Almond on December 1 that they must retreat to preserve the security of their commands and to extend the supply lines of the enemy [12] —if his bombers were not permitted to go to the enemy in Manchuria an American retreat would serve to draw the enemy within the regions open to American bombers.

85

B

On December 3 General MacArthur sent the Joint Chiefs a lengthy statement in which he first explained why he believed that it was impractical logistically to unite the Eighth Army and the X Corps in the narrow neck of North Korea. MacArthur then warned his superiors that 'unless ground reinforcements of the greatest magnitude are promptly supplied, this Command will be either forced into successive withdrawals with diminished powers of resistance after each such move, or will be forced to take up beachhead bastion positions which, while insuring a degree of prolonged resistance, would afford little hope of anything beyond defense.'

Indeed, even more alarmingly, MacArthur went on to add that 'unless some positive and immediate action is taken, hopes for success cannot be justified and steady attrition leading to final destruction can reasonably be contemplated.' Winding up with a gloomy judgment on the condition of his still understrength divisions, MacArthur called for new 'political decisions and strategic plans in implementation thereof, adequate fully to meet the realities involved.'

Upon receipt of this message, President Truman ordered General Collins to visit the Far East to check on the circumstances actually prevailing. At the same time the Joint Chiefs replied to MacArthur's message as follows: 'We consider that the preservation of your forces is now the primary consideration. Consolidation of forces into beachheads is concurred in.' [13]

Meanwhile, in Washington another issue had arisen to perplex the Administration, an issue on which publicly, at least, General MacArthur had the good sense to avoid comment. After having denied, in a press conference held on November 30, that the United States would abandon its mission in Korea, in response to a provocative question President Truman then said that there always was consideration of the use of atomic bombs, although he personally did not want to employ them. Further explanations did not extricate the President from the probably accidental implication of his reply,[14] and the result was an anxious debate in the British House of Commons, not only over the possible employment of nuclear weapons, but also on the whole question of how far the war in the Far East should be extended. The Canadian Minister of External Affairs, Lester Pearson, was already advocating making peace with Communist China by 'every means.'[15]

During the parliamentary debate in Britain Winston Churchill observed: 'It is one of the most well-known—almost hackneyed—strategical and tactical methods to draw your opponents' reserves to one part of the field and then, at the right moment, to strike in another.... [Thus] the United Nations should avoid by every means in their power becoming entangled inextricably in a war with China.... For it is in Europe that the world cause will be decided ... it is there that the mortal danger lies.' With characteristic magnanimity, however, Churchill urged his Labour party opponents not to criticize MacArthur personally, both on account of the gravity of the crisis and because of the relatively small British contribution to the Korean War.[16]

Prime Minister Attlee finally relieved parliamentary tension by announcing his intention to fly to Washington to see President Truman about these issues. In his meeting with the President between December 4 and 7, certain divergencies between the British and American positions became apparent. Mr. Attlee, for example, regarded the Chinese Communists as fairly independent of Russian con-

87

trol and already ripe for Titoist ideas; on the other hand, once burned in China, the Americans united in considering Red China as a thoroughgoing Soviet satellite, although Secretary Acheson foresaw that the Chinese Communists would probably act in the same way in any event, whether satellites or not. The Americans assured Mr. Attlee that, while few of the President's advisers favored an all-out war with Red China to regain North Korea, the United States would still evacuate South Korea only as a consequence of military necessity. In short, after a brief flirtation with the terrifying potentialities of a policy of liberation, a chastened, uncertain, but still stubborn Democratic Administration was returning to its true love—containment.

Since containment was, in essence, the *raison d'être* of the NATO military alliance—shortly to be fleshed out with real military strength under a new supreme commander, Gen. Dwight D. Eisenhower—the British could easily agree with this basic American conclusion. The military concomitant of a policy of containment in Korea was, of course, to be found only in a limited land war. Both sides recognized the difficulties with American public opinion in such a policy, particularly with American nationalists, who, in Mr. Truman's scathing phrase, 'saw nothing wrong in plunging headlong into an Asian war but would raise no finger for the defense of Europe; who thought a British Prime Minister was never to be trusted but Chiang Kai-shek could do no wrong.' [17]

In opposing any attempt to buy the Chinese Communists out of the war with Formosa or other such diplomatic inducements, in practice Secretary Acheson was probably recognizing the strength of American nationalist sympathies with Chiang Kai-shek more than the futility of concessions to the Communists. Nevertheless the Administration remained boxed within a rather narrow range of possibilities if it was to conciliate both domestic and NATO opinion. Secretary Acheson now favored negotiating a cease-fire in Korea in the future rather than immediately, as General MacArthur had already advocated.

In their final communiqué the President and the Prime Minister accepted the idea of a negotiated peace and, more obliquely, of its corollary, the loss of North Korea to the Chinese Communists. In effect, Truman and Attlee also announced their agreement not to employ nuclear weapons in Korea without further consultation between the two principal NATO Allies.[18] The President's decision here may have been encouraged by the opinion of experts that there were no Korean targets important enough to justify using the still scarce atom bomb. At the same time the political danger to the American reputation in Asia of another Hiroshima would obviously have been enormous.[19] But the fact remains that, since the United States did not dare employ nuclear weapons at a time when it had almost a monopoly of such methods, for most practical purposes the strategic creed eventually to be called Massive Retaliation was dead three full years before it would officially be proclaimed.[20]

In accord with the subsequent position of the Republican party in the United States, the leader of the Conservative opposition in Britain, Winston Churchill, criticized the Truman-Attlee announcement on this occasion because it precluded a United States bluff or threat to employ nuclear weapons.[21] Still, it may be seen why Mr. Attlee would conclude about President Truman, a trifle smugly: '[He was] one of the best. He didn't know much to start, but he learned very quickly.'[22] Once again the Americans

89

were being educated in the terms of limited war—both in its obvious and in its more subtle terms—by the traditional proponents of such an attitude toward war and life.

Whether the Truman-Attlee conference constituted the deliberate turning point of the Korean War, as certain well-informed critics have suggested,[23] or whether the decision of the conferees in favor of a limited war in the Far East simply reflected the only route which the Truman Administration could find out of its political dilemma, is, in the light of evidence so far available, still an open question. Even at the time, however, suspecting more than met the eye, a majority of the Senate Republicans demanded the right of concurrence in any Administration agreement with the British.[24]

Meanwhile, in Tokyo, General MacArthur's growing chagrin over his defeat in North Korea—and particularly over the unpleasant comments [25] in the previously friendly American press on his supposed role in this defeat—had evoked a series of interviews between the thin-skinned [26] General and various U.S. news agencies. Denying that his strategy had caused the Red Chinese assault, claiming that he had no warnings of this attack, complaining of being forced to operate under the handicap of 'enormous' limitations 'without precedent in military history,' MacArthur lashed out against what he termed 'misleading anonymous gossip' which he said had already reached the U.S. troops in Korea.[27]

Embarrassed by MacArthur's public rejoinders during the delicate conferences with the British, on December 6 the Administration may have nipped in the bud another provocative announcement on the part of MacArthur by sending out a directive through the Joint Chiefs, ostensibly directed to all field commanders, that they should exercise 'extreme caution in public statements.' Theater commanders were further enjoined to refrain 'from direct communication on military or foreign policy with newspapers, magazines or other publicity media in the United States.' State or Defense Department approval was required for all future releases.[28] At the same time the J.C.S. warned all commanders that they considered the situation in Korea had greatly increased the possibility of a general war. Accordingly, they directed such commanders to augment their readiness as much as possible without creating an atmosphere of alarm. Among the many activities resulting from this war warning, the U.S. Mediterranean Fleet promptly went to sea.[29] As the British and American conferees in Washington were concluding, the ramifications of the Korean War were truly international.

More privately, from a report made by General Collins following his trip to the Far East, the Administration was also being acquainted with MacArthur's views. MacArthur told Collins that a continuation of the J.C.S. limitations on his actions in face of the Chinese Communist attack 'would represent essentially a surrender. Under these conditions the question of an armistice would be a political matter, helpful but not essential from a military standpoint. Our forces would have to be withdrawn from Korea, but we should not be precipitate in seeking an armistice . . .' Disheartened by defeat, MacArthur now supported an armistice along the 38th parallel, should the Chinese Communists be willing to accept such terms.[30]

As an alternative to such an armistice MacArthur advocated a full-fledged program of retaliation against the Chinese Communists. In brief, he favored an exploitation of the American sea-air superiority by bombing and blockading Communist China. At the same time he de-

91

sired to employ Chinese Nationalist troops both in Korea and to assault South China in order to divert the Red Chinese from Korea.

It was this last suggestion which most distressed President Truman. Disinclined to support Chiang Kai-shek any more than was essential, Mr. Truman felt that American support for a Chinese Nationalist attack on South China would be 'an act of war.' Perhaps somewhat more objectively, the President also believed that bombing Red China would harden Chinese opinion against the United States, while a blockade which did not cut the Trans-Siberian railroad would be ineffective. President Truman concluded that General MacArthur was willing to risk a general war; in his own opinion, at least, Mr. Truman was not.[31]

At a meeting of the National Security Council on December 11, the President agreed that, if necessary, there should be a gradual withdrawal from Korea, a withdrawal to be dictated by military rather than political considerations. The issue was pressing, since at this time two of MacArthur's aides expected that the United States would be driven entirely out of the Korean peninsula. Gen. Bedell Smith doubted a Russian entry into the war should the United States mobilize fully. As usual, General Marshall stressed the importance of strengthening rather than frightening Western Europe with American policy.[32]

Three days later, the United Nations offered the Chinese Communists a cease-fire along the 38th parallel, an offer which the Red Chinese, who now anticipated a complete victory in Korea, would soon reject. Since diplomacy in the United Nations and a Presidential Proclamation of a National Emergency on December 16 had both failed to prevent the triumphant Chinese Communists from crossing the 38th parallel in the wake of the retreating U.N. forces, the Truman Administration was again faced with the threat of a complete American defeat in Korea.[33]

At this dismal moment the U.S. Eighth Army Commander, Lt. Gen. Walton Walker, was killed in a jeep accident. His successor, Lt. Gen. Matthew Ridgway, began his memorable campaign to combat declining morale among his men by announcing that hereafter real estate was 'incidental' to tactical operations in Korea.[34] Real estate might indeed be incidental to any operations in Korea when the possibility of evacuating the entire peninsula was the great issue at hand—an evacuation which would be comparable to Dunkirk in scale and loss of prestige.

On December 29, with the phenomenally successful evacuation of the U.S. X Corps from Hungnam freshly in mind, the Joint Chiefs informed MacArthur that it appeared 'from estimates available' that the Chinese Communists had the strength to force a total United States withdrawal from Korea. While the Joint Chiefs still felt that the United Nations should attempt to hang on in Korea if this could be done without serious losses, the J.C.S. again warned MacArthur that, in the face of the increased threat of general war, he could not expect further American ground troops as reinforcements. The J.C.S. went on to give MacArthur their view that in any event a major war should not be fought in Korea, a partial anticipation of General Bradley's famous subsequent indictment of MacArthur's program as the wrong war. Finally MacArthur's opinions on the evacuation issue were requested because, as the J.C.S. emphasized, MacArthur's primary mission remained the defense of Japan.[35]

Since there were no American troops left for this newly stressed primary mission in Japan, plainly MacArthur was being given a strong incentive to favor the evacuation of all his forces from Korea. The bitterness of the General and his staff officers on this issue can thus be well understood, but certainly not MacArthur's later assertion that his disagreement was only with the Administration and not with the Joint Chiefs of Staff.[36]

MacArthur's reply on December 30 again advocated the bombing and blockade of Red China as well as the employment of Chinese Nationalists against Peiping. On this last matter, at least briefly, General Ridgway would support MacArthur. The Supreme Commander explained that he did not feel any new American action could further aggravate the situation so far as Communist China alone was concerned. With respect to the Soviet Union, MacArthur wrote that the Russians would act on the basis of their own estimate with little regard to other factors. MacArthur warned that any termination of the Korean campaign would release Red Chinese forces for action elsewhere. He concluded with perhaps the most effective and reasoned criticism he would ever employ against the European proclivities of the Administration.

> I understand thoroughly the demand for European security and fully concur in doing everything possible in that sector, but not to the point of accepting defeat anywhere else—an acceptance which I am sure could not fail to insure later defeat in Europe itself. The preparations for the defense of Europe, however, by the most optimistic estimate are aimed at a condition of readiness two years hence. The use of forces in the present emergency in the Far East could not in any way prejudice this basic concept. To the contrary, it would ensure thoroughly seasoned forces for later commitment in Europe synchronously with Europe's own development of military resources.[37]

94

Perhaps the new emphasis upon defending Japan and certainly his own pessimism concerning the training and morale of the South Koreans affected MacArthur's reply to a query from the Joint Chiefs. When asked by them whether he could gain reinforcements by arming the South Koreans, MacArthur replied on January 6 that he preferred instead to equip the Japanese National Police Reserve.[38] The J.C.S. were not alone in losing hope for the South Koreans at this juncture.

On January 5, Senator Robert Taft, in effect, had also called for the evacuation of Korea. As always, Taft preferred an isolationist Republican emphasis upon sea and air power, leaving to foreigners the maintenance of large armies and large campaigns on land. Within another nine months Taft would have completed the full circle from his initial qualified approval of the United States intervention in Korea, in October 1951 terming the struggle there 'an unnecessary war.' In January 1951 Senators Bridges and Wherry also expressed views similar to those of Taft, skillfully concealing their disillusionment with the Korean War by suggesting evacuation of the peninsula only as an alternative to further aid for General MacArthur.[39]

At last, on January 9, MacArthur received a definite reply from the Joint Chiefs and the President to his message of December 30. For the time being his retaliatory measures were turned down all along the line, although continued consideration of them was promised for the future. His primary mission remained the defense of Japan, to which he must retreat if faced with severe losses of men and matériel in attempting to hold a Korean bridgehead. Stronger blockade action against the Chinese Communists depended upon current negotiations with the

95

British. Finally, MacArthur might not attack Red China with either American or Chinese Nationalist forces without a prior enemy action against the United States outside of Korea. As a consolation prize MacArthur was offered the possibility in the future of two additional partly trained U.S. National Guard Divisions.[40]

MacArthur answered the Joint Chiefs the next day with a long defensive communication in which he said that he was too weak to hold both Korea and Japan, although he might maintain 'a beachhead line' for 'a limited time' in Korea. Whether his losses in this process would be severe would to some extent 'depend upon the connotation one gives the term.' He said that his troops, 'embittered by the shameful propaganda which has falsely condemned their fighting qualities and courage in [a] misunderstood retrograde maneuver,' were also 'tired from a long and difficult campaign.' Excluding any overriding political considerations, and given the limitations imposed upon him by the Joint Chiefs, MacArthur indicated that his command should be evacuated from Korea 'as rapidly as it is feasible tactically to do so.' Should it be politically necessary to stay on in Korea, he would do so regardless of the risk to Japan and 'whatever casualties [might] result' up to the 'complete destruction' of his command.[41]

In the light of this desperate, but fortunately inaccurate appraisal—a consequence no doubt intended by MacArthur—the Joint Chiefs considered a series of stronger actions against Communist China, a series of which MacArthur's own proposals were to form a part. Meanwhile the General was told to stall on evacuation in order to hurt the enemy as much as possible and to gain time for United States diplomatic consultation with her Allies. The J.C.S. now agreed with the supposed position of MacArthur at this time, namely that it was 'unfeasible under existing conditions' to stay indefinitely in Korea.[42]

Greatly disturbed, and feeling that he must penetrate the barrier of MacArthur's staff [43] to warn the General about the political implications of American policy, President Truman sent the General a personal letter of explanation on January 13. The President must have had some difficulty in formulating his political objectives, since the State Department preferred to postpone establishing its objectives until the military situation was clearer, while not unnaturally the Joint Chiefs desired the converse.

Moreover, to the great disgust of the Republicans in Congress, the Administration was showing signs of a willingness to abandon Formosa as well as Korea for the sake of maintaining support in the United Nations.[44]

The core of the President's letter to MacArthur read:

> Our courses of action at this time should be such as to consolidate the great majority of the United Nations. This majority is not merely part of the organization but is also the nations whom we would desperately need to count on as allies in the event the Soviet Union moves against us. Further, pending the build-up of our national strength, we must act with great prudence insofar as extending the area of hostilities is concerned. Steps which might in themselves be fully justified and which might lend some assistance to the campaign in Korea would not be beneficial if they thereby involved Japan or Western Europe in large-scale hostilities.
>
> We recognize, of course, that continued resistance might not be militarily possible with the limited forces with which you are being called upon to meet large Chinese armies. Further, in the present world situation, your forces must be preserved as an effective instrument for the defense of Japan and elsewhere.... In the worst case, it would be important that, if we must withdraw from Korea, it be clear to the

world that that course is forced upon us by military necessity and that we shall not accept the result politically or militarily until the aggression has been rectified.

In reaching a final decision about Korea, I shall have to give constant thought to the main threat from the Soviet Union and to the need for a rapid expansion of our Armed Forces to meet this great danger.

The President concluded his letter with another balm for the sensibilities of his unhappy warrior: 'The entire nation is grateful for your splendid leadership in the difficult struggle in Korea and for the superb performance of your forces under the most difficult circumstances.' [45]

Under these circumstances two members of the Joint Chiefs, General Collins and Vandenberg, were ordered to visit Korea to ascertain the situation there for themselves. According to the account of one of MacArthur's aides, the latter decided the U.N. forces should hold on in Korea when he received the President's political explanation on January 14. If this is true, perhaps it was because MacArthur now hoped that the Joint Chiefs were about to accept his program against Communist China as a part of their own contemplated sixteen point study in this same direction. General Collins, however, remained less certain of the chances of remaining in Korea until he had made a visit to the front on January 17. Then he reported to the President that the Red Chinese advance had been stopped and that the morale of the U.S. Eighth Army was being rapidly restored under General Ridgway's leadership. But even before his visit to the front, Collins had publicly announced that as far as Korea was concerned the Americans were 'going to stay and fight.' [46] By January 20, MacArthur, too, had publicly concluded that 'no one is going to drive us into the sea.' [47]

The great evacuation threat had subsided and with it the Joint Chiefs' interest in extending the war with China. But hereafter General MacArthur either believed, or simulated the belief, that he had won the Joint Chiefs over to his program in whole or in part, as somewhat earlier he had won over General Ridgway on the diversionary use of Chinese Nationalists, following the latter's arrival in the Far East in late December.[48]

VIII

The Recall

February 1 — April 11, 1951

'I feel that the fate of the nation depends on me, and I feel that I have not one single friend at the seat of the government. Any day may bring an order relieving me from my command. If they simply let me alone I feel sure of success, but will they do it?' [1]

—Gen. George McClellan, May 3, 1862

'You are not to decide, discuss or confer [with the enemy] on any political questions; such questions the President holds in his own hands, and will submit them to no military conferences or conventions.' [2]

—Lincoln's instructions to Grant, March 1865

'I became so fed up with the way things were being conducted I thought I could do more outside the service than in it. . . .' [3]

—Gen. William Mitchell, March 12, 1926

'I wasn't one of the great Presidents, but I had a good time trying to be one, I can tell you that.' [4]

—Harry S. Truman in 1959

Under strong American pressure, but with considerable reluctance, especially on the part of its Asian members, on February 1 the United Nations General Assembly condemned Communist China for her entry into Korea. The United States' NATO Allies had supported the American position in the United Nations only with the reservation that they would oppose almost any further action in Korea.[5]

On the other hand, in Tokyo General MacArthur had already asked publicly three times to bomb what he now called 'the privileged sanctuary of Manchuria.'[6] More privately, according to the not always completely reliable General Whitney, MacArthur now favored supplementing a United Nations advance, which had commenced in mid-February, with vast amphibious landings on both coasts of North Korea, after cutting the enemy supply lines with radioactive waste.[7] The J.C.S. themselves were torn between accepting the possibility of a military stalemate in Korea and taking steps to defeat the Chinese Communists in Korea alone—this last was a compromise course of action which might offend General MacArthur and the NATO Allies about equally.

Although both President Truman and General Bradley issued statements on February 16 to the effect that MacArthur had the 'complete confidence' of the Administration and would retain a high degree of freedom of action to run the war without undue interference from Washington,[8] the General was no longer to be satisfied with Administration flattery. He could read Secretary Marshall's statement of the same day that the Democratic

Administration intended to send four American divisions to General Eisenhower's NATO command in Europe at a time when his requests for further reinforcements were being rejected.[9] Moreover, he had now gained another influential and newly vocal advocate in Congress, Republican Minority Leader Joseph Martin.

On February 12, Congressman Martin delivered a speech in New York in which he said that the Administration was preventing 800,000 Chinese Nationalists on Formosa from opening 'a second front in Asia,' a highly fanciful figure which Martin then contrasted with the distasteful reality of 200,000 American combat troops in Korea. In what appears to have been a leak concerning the Joint Chiefs' consideration of desperate remedies during the evacuation crisis of the previous month, Martin declared that responsible opinion in the Pentagon favored such a Chinese Nationalist offensive as achieving that isolationist beau ideal, 'the cheapest operation' the United States could promote in Asia. Congressman Martin continued: 'If we are not in Korea to win, then this [Truman] Administration should be indicted for the murder of thousands of American boys.' Joseph Martin was not, of course, the first American in the Puritan tradition to feel that limitations on war constituted murder.

Even more ominously for the Administration, Congressman Martin added: 'There is good reason to believe that General MacArthur favors such an operation' on the part of the Chinese Nationalists, but in Martin's opinion 'the same State Department crowd that cut off aid' to Nationalist China in 1946 was now resisting employing the Nationalists, since this would imply that they had been wrong on Chiang Kai-shek in the earlier period. Raising his sights somewhat, the Republican Minority Leader concluded enthusiastically: 'If we want a strategy that will save Europe and save Asia at the same time . . . we must clean out the State Department from the top to bottom, starting with Dean Acheson.' [10]

Whatever the conditions at the front, the stalemate between the Administration and General MacArthur continued. It may be recalled that during another stalemate on another peninsula—Bataan—in the opinion of one critic, General MacArthur had tried 'to goad' President Roosevelt into sending him more aid by suggesting that the Filipinos felt betrayed 'in favor of others.' When Roosevelt proved incapable of responding as MacArthur desired, the General had then decided that the President was his 'arch foe.' [11]

On February 21, General MacArthur was informed by the Joint Chiefs that he still might not bomb Racin, an important Chinese Communist supply center in Korea near the Soviet border. In a report on February 23, MacArthur complained of the 'unparalleled conditions of restraint and handicap' imposed on his forces. On March 1, the request of MacArthur's Far Eastern Air Force to bomb the generating plants on the Yalu River frontier of China was disapproved.[12] On March 7, to the embarrassment of the American representatives at the United Nations, General MacArthur announced that any further U.N. advance on land would involve a 'savage slaughter' [13] and would 'militarily benefit the enemy more than it would ourselves.' MacArthur's statement finished: 'Vital decisions have yet to be made—decisions far beyond the scope of the authority vested in me as the military commander, decisions which are neither solely political nor solely military, but which must provide on the highest international levels an answer to the obscurities which now becloud the unsolved problems raised by Red China's undeclared war in Korea.' [14] Gen. Matthew Ridgway's assertion on March 12 to the effect that reaching the 38th parallel would constitute a 'tremendous victory' for the United Nations,[15] made a striking contrast to MacArthur's views—especially to the harassed Administration in Washington.

To be sure, procrastination on the part of both the Joint Chiefs of Staff and the State Department had prevented any revision of MacArthur's basic directive. As American divisions, freshly brought up to strength and with ever higher morale, recaptured Seoul, the Korean capital, in mid-March, General MacArthur's basic directive still read that, while he should hurt the Communists as severely as possible in Korea, he must limit his activities to protect the security of his command and of his Japanese base. As Senator Leverett Saltonstall later suggested, this was an unnecessarily 'negative policy,' stemming from a period of defeat. Moreover, it was particularly negative since, according to General Collins, Japan would shortly be safe in any event with two new American divisions, with U.S. naval and air forces, and with her own recently enlarged para-military National Police Reserve.[16] It is apparent why the intensity of General MacArthur's frustration was increasing; and his subsequent assertion before the Senate Hearings that the Administration had 'no policy ... no plan or anything' [17] for Korea becomes more intelligible in this context.

Meanwhile the approach of the U.N. forces to the 38th parallel was evoking a strong reaction in favor of negotiating with the enemy among those U.N. members with troops in Korea. This finally compelled the Administration to make a firmer decision on its own future course of action in the peninsula. In effect, the Truman Administration, again half-hearted, decided to go along with its Allies rather than with MacArthur, although its decision still may have been neither explicit nor absolutely final. But without question it may be concluded that, along with its fellow NATO Allies, since the American defeat in December 1950, Washington had lost any interest in driving back to the Yalu. Unlike its Allies, the Administration was willing to advance again some distance beyond the 38th parallel to establish a strong military line for the sake of subsequent diplomatic bargaining.[18]

In any event, on March 20 the Joint Chiefs of Staff sent General MacArthur the following message:

> State Department planning a Presidential announcement shortly that, with clearing of bulk of South Korea of aggressors, United Nations now preparing to discuss conditions of settlement in Korea. Strong U.N. feeling exists that further diplomatic efforts toward settlement should be made before any advance with major forces north of 38th parallel. Time will be required to determine diplomatic reactions and permit new negotiations that may develop. Recognizing that parallel has no military significance, State has asked J.C.S. what authority you should have to permit sufficient freedom of action for next few weeks to provide security for U.N. forces and maintain contact with enemy. Your recommendation desired.[19]

General MacArthur answered the J.C.S. message on March 21. The General requested merely that no further limitations be imposed upon his command. Astonishingly, considering the nature of a message well designed to drive him frantic, MacArthur felt that his current directive covered the situation quite well. But given the limitations placed upon him, he did not expect to be able to clear North Korea.[20]

Whether it was General MacArthur's final loss of hope for the support or at least acquiescence of the Administration with regard to his own program; whether, in actuality, the General sensed that the Joint Chiefs, as Joint Chiefs do, would follow the political weathervane away from the direction of what had been too personal a victory in Korea; whether, as two of his admirers have suggested, the General was deliberating risking his career for the sake of thwarting a negotiated peace; whether the absolutist and perfectionist tenor of his personality since West Point days had called forth this reaction in spite of himself; or whether he was at least trying to gain credit for the peace negotiations in lieu of an obvious victory—[21] it is at present impossible to speak with assurance of the motives of the General. But MacArthur's own explanation that his defiant statement of March 24 was no more than an instrument of psychological warfare,[22] aimed at his enemies in Korea rather than in Washington, seems inadequate, to say the least.

In the statement which, according to Mr. Truman, brought about his decision to dismiss MacArthur from his command, the General declared:

> Operations continue to schedule and plan. We have now substantially cleared South Korea of organized Communist forces ...
>
> Of even greater significance than our tactical successes has been the clear revelation that this new enemy, Red China, of such exaggerated and vaunted military power, lacks the industrial capacity to provide adequately many critical items necessary to the conduct of modern war. He lacks the manufacturing base and those raw materials needed to produce, maintain and operate even moderate air and naval power, and he cannot provide the essentials for successful ground

operations, such as tanks, heavy artillery and other refinements science has introduced into the conduct of military campaigns. Formerly his great numerical potential might well have filled this gap, but with the development of existing methods of mass destruction, numbers alone do not offset the vulnerability inherent in such deficiencies. Control of the seas and the air, which in turn means control over supplies, communications, and transportation, are no less essential and decisive now than in the past. When this control exists as in our case, and is coupled with an inferiority of ground fire power as in the enemy's case, the resulting disparity is such that it cannot be overcome by bravery, however fanatical, or the most gross indifference to human loss.

These military weaknesses have been clearly and definitely revealed since Red China entered upon its undeclared war in Korea. Even under the inhibitions which now restrict the activity of the United Nations forces and the corresponding military advantages which accrue to Red China, it has been shown its complete inability to accomplish by force of arms the conquest of Korea. The enemy, therefore, must by now be painfully aware that a decision of the United Nations to depart from its tolerant effort to contain the war to the area of Korea, through an expansion of our military operations to its coastal areas and interior bases, would doom Red China to the risk of imminent military collapse. These basic facts being established, there should be no insuperable difficulty in arriving at decisions on the Korean problem if the issues are resolved on their own merits, without being burdened by extraneous matters not directly related to Korea, such as Formosa or China's seat in the United Nations.

The Korean nation and people, which have been so cruelly ravaged, must not be sacrificed. This is a paramount concern. Apart from the military area of the problem where issues are resolved in the course of combat, the fundamental questions continue to be political in nature and must find their answer in the diplomatic sphere. Within the area of my authority as the military commander, however, it would be needless to say that I stand ready at any time to confer in the field with the commander-in-chief of the enemy forces in the earnest effort to find any military means whereby realization of the political objectives of the United Nations in Korea, to which no nation may justly take exception, might be accomplished without further bloodshed.[23]

On the same day on which MacArthur released this de facto public ultimatum to the Administration, President Truman met his advisers to consider how to handle the problem. Queries were pouring in from Allied capitals regarding the significance of the apparent shift in American policy, signalized in the words of the Norwegian Ambassador by MacArthur's 'pronunciamento.' [24]

Indeed, MacArthur had actually determined American policy, if only temporarily. For the time being the State Department was forced to abandon its efforts made with thirteen other Allied nations to negotiate a settlement of the Korean conflict. In Mr. Acheson's graphic explanation, a Presidential statement was now impossible since the field of negotiations 'had been occupied' by General MacArthur. Furthermore, in the State Department view, MacArthur's speech might be considered an implied threat to extend the war into China. The Department hurriedly released a statement saying that General MacArthur had gone beyond his responsibilities as a field commander and that the diplomatic issues involved were still being handled by intergovernmental consultations.[25]

After a discussion with the President and State Department regarding the meaning of the President's directive of December 6 which required the checking of important public statements on the part of theater commanders

through Washington prior to their release, the Joint Chiefs
sent MacArthur the following directive:

From J.C.S. Personal for MacArthur

The President has directed that your attention be called
to his order as transmitted 6 December 1950. In view of the
information given you 20 March 1951 any further statements
by you must be coordinated as prescribed in the order of
6 December.

The President has also directed that in the event Communist military leaders request an armistice in the field, you
immediately report that fact to the J.C.S. for instructions.

Bradley [26]

On the next day, March 25, apparently oblivious to
the impact of General MacArthur's announcement, *The
Sunday Times* in Great Britain noted that negotiations between the West and the Chinese Communists were about
to take place on the basis of a military stabilization with
no unification of the Korean peninsula. On March 26,
General MacArthur's early February report was submitted
to the United Nations. In it the General had stressed that
his forces were 'still engaged in a war of maneuver' and
that 'the concept advanced by some that we should establish a line across Korea and enter the positional war is
wholly unrealistic and illusory.' In fact, MacArthur claimed
such warfare 'would insure destruction of our forces piece-
meal.' In February the General had also professed to
believe that talk of crossing the 38th parallel was 'purely
academic.' [27]

Academic or otherwise, on March 27 MacArthur's
Korean troops quietly crossed the parallel. Only on April 3
were the South Koreans followed by regular U.N. forces,
Washington carefully specifying, however, that this was
not to constitute a general advance into North Korea.[28]

It is possible that, in spite of MacArthur's open defiance on March 24 and the hardening determination of President Truman to recall him which resulted, this new crisis in American civil-military relations might in time have blown over. At this point, however, a final element in the drama reappeared—the deus ex machina of the last scenes of MacArthur's active military career, House Minority Leader Joseph Martin.

On March 8 Martin had written MacArthur in the following vein of mingled cajolery and provocation:

My dear General: In the current discussions on foreign policy and overall strategy many of us have been distressed that, although the European aspects have been heavily emphasized, we have been without the views of yourself as Commander in Chief of the Far Eastern Command.

I think it is imperative to the security of our Nation and for the safety of the world that policies of the United States embrace the broadest possible strategy, and that in our earnest desire to protect Europe, we not weaken our position in Asia.

Enclosed is a copy of an address I delivered in Brooklyn, N.Y., February 12, stressing this vital point and suggesting that the forces of Generalissimo Chiang Kai-shek on Formosa might be employed in the opening of a second Asiatic front to relieve the pressure on our forces in Korea.

I have since repeated the essence of this thesis in other speeches, and intend to do so again on March 21, when I will be on a radio hook-up.

I would deem it a great help if I could have your views on this point, either on a confidential basis or otherwise. Your admirers are legion, and the respect you command is enormous. May success be yours in the gigantic undertaking which you direct.

Sincerely yours,
Joseph W. Martin, Jr.[29]

Perhaps mindful of his directive of December 6, General MacArthur, it should be noted, did not answer Martin's letter until March 20, the same day on which he had been sent definite word from the Joint Chiefs of the rejection of his program. General Whitney records that the official J.C.S. message did not reach Tokyo until March 21, but the General may well have had some anticipation of it in advance. In any event, according to Whitney, MacArthur answered Martin's letter simply as part of his routine practice with Congressmen.[30]

Hon. Joseph W. Martin, Jr.
House of Representatives, Washington, D.C.

Dear Congressman Martin: I am most grateful for your note of the 8th forwarding me a copy of your address of February 12. The latter I have read with much interest, and find that with the passage of years you have certainly lost none of your old-time punch.

My views and recommendations with respect to the situation created by Red China's entry into the war against us in Korea have been submitted to Washington in most complete detail. Generally these views are well known and clearly understood, as they follow the conventional pattern of meeting force with maximum counter-force, as we have never failed to do in the past. Your view with respect to the utilization of the Chinese forces on Formosa is in conflict with neither logic nor this tradition.

It seems strangely difficult for some to realize that here in Asia is where the Communist conspirators have elected to make their play for global conquest, and that we have joined the issue thus raised on the battlefield; that here we fight Europe's war with arms while the diplomats there still fight it with words; that if we lose this war to Communism in Asia the fall of Europe is inevitable; win it and Europe most probably would avoid war and yet preserve freedom. As you

113

pointed out, we must win. There is no substitute for victory.

With renewed thanks and expressions of most cordial regard I am,

> Faithfully yours,
> Douglas MacArthur [31]

Seven years before, in 1944, another Republican leader in Congress, hopeful of grooming MacArthur as presidential timber, had found his plans abruptly deflated as a result of the injudicious replies which the General had dictated in response to the letter of another congressman. At that time MacArthur had described his intemperate messages as merely 'amiable acknowledgments' of a congressman's correspondence; a skillful politician such as Senator Vandenberg knew better when he sadly noted in 1944: 'If he [MacArthur] hadn't written them [those letters] [Congressman] Miller couldn't have used them.' [32]

As another adept practitioner of the gentle art of politics, Harry Truman, would remark in 1958: 'It's too bad that the General didn't have a good political adviser. If he'd have [sic] consulted me about what he ought to do, I would have made it much easier for him, and he'd be a much more popular man than he is today.' [33] Popularity may not have been, however, what Douglas MacArthur was directly courting when he reacted to Congressman Martin's tempting bait—his ethos was derived from an earlier era, from what his admirer, Field Marshal Lord Alanbrooke, has termed the attitude of a 'grand seigneur' rather than from a more democratic tradition of personal conduct. With respect to MacArthur's role in Korea, Alanbrooke has further added: 'To my mind, a general who is not prepared to assume some responsibility, on his own, when unable to obtain political direction, is of little value.' [34]

After waiting ten days, purportedly to see whether General MacArthur would request that his letter be withheld, on April 5 Representative Martin read the general's message on the floor of the House. Martin explained that he 'owed it to the American people to tell them the information I had from a great and reliable source.' When asked whether the J.C.S. reminder of March 24, bringing his attention to the restrictions on his public utterances of December 6, would have affected him if it had reached him before he wrote Martin, MacArthur conceded that it might have had some influence—subsequently his most ardent supporters have doubted it.[35]

In the words of Defense Secretary Marshall, General MacArthur's letter to Congressman Martin was no more than one of an 'accumulation' of incidents which 'brought ... to a head' the issue of the General's continued status as United Nations Commander in the Far East. President Truman, in fact, has said that he had objected much more to MacArthur's letter to the Veterans of Foreign Wars of the previous August. After all, in the Martin letter European diplomats were MacArthur's principal target rather than that Achilles' heel of Truman Administration foreign policy before the Korean War—the Communist conquest of the Chinese mainland.[36] Nevertheless, the letter to Martin had precipitated the problem of who was conducting American policy even more inescapably than MacArthur's challenge of March 24; the Administration could no longer procrastinate on insults of such a flagrant order on the part of one of its principal agents.

The day following the release of MacArthur's letter, April 6, the President met with several of his advisers to discuss what to do; in his memoirs Mr. Truman says that he was careful not to influence his colleagues by disclosing that he had already decided to recall MacArthur.

Averell Harriman first expressed the opinion that Mr. Truman should have fired MacArthur two years earlier on the grounds of some unnamed insubordination even before the Korean War. Defense Secretary Marshall, however, advised careful consideration of the whole issue, observing that MacArthur's relief might create difficulties for military appropriations in Congress. General Bradley saw the question as entirely a matter of military discipline and also thought that MacArthur should be relieved for insubordination. The Republicans' *bête noire*, Secretary of State Acheson, likewise believed that MacArthur should be recalled, but with Marshall he advised caution, saying: 'If you relieve MacArthur, you will have the biggest fight of your Administration.' Mr. Acheson further recommended that the President obtain the unanimous advice of the Joint Chiefs of Staff before acting.[37]

In view of the relative forbearance of the Secretary of State, Mr. Acheson's denial that the United States' NATO Allies caused MacArthur's relief seems valid.[38] In any event, between April 5 and April 9 there was not much time for heavy foreign pressure to be mobilized. To be sure, on April 7, British Minister of State Kenneth Younger referred publicly to 'such irresponsible statements as seem to come out at frequent intervals from highly placed quarters, without the authority of the United Nations, or indeed of any member Government.' According to *The Observer* of London on April 8, Mr. Younger's statement was only a mild version of the true sentiments of the British Government. In what may have been an official leak, *The Observer* said that the British Government had already taken 'the strongest possible exception' to MacArthur's letter to Martin, which it interpreted 'as foreshadowing an extension of the war to the mainland of Asia.' The British Embassy in Washington had supposedly asked how MacArthur could make statements at such complete variance with the foreign policy of the United States Government.[39]

Of course the British conception of the role of an officer on active service was very different from that of the American Puritan ideology, with its stress upon the total divorce of the military and political components of power; nonetheless, *The Observer* had scored several points which no American Administration could afford to gainsay. On at least one issue it is interesting to see that the British Government was in apparent agreement with General Mac-Arthur at this time; both doubted whether the Russians wanted war at present, basing their point on the supposed weakness of the Soviets and their lack of sufficient incentive.[40] As so often in the Washington debate hereafter, the British Government and General MacArthur had reached opposing conclusions concerning what to do, notwithstanding their agreement on at least one basic postulate.

In Washington on April 7, at a meeting of top Administration officials, Secretary of Defense Marshall said that after reading through the past evidence of General Mac-Arthur's activities he now agreed that MacArthur should have been recalled two years earlier. There then ensued some discussion of the suggestion—perhaps politically too clever—that MacArthur be deprived only of his responsibility for the Korean War, while retaining his post as Supreme Commander in Japan. Eventually, as Secretary Marshall explained, this plausible idea was dropped as impractical, since it was too difficult to divide authority between the fighting front in Korea and the main American operating base in Japan.[41] Certainly the notable experiment involving MacArthur in a divided over-all command at Leyte Gulf in 1944 had helped bring about results which nobody cared to contemplate again.[42] Finally, in accordance with Secretary Acheson's adept advice, the President requested the opinion of the Joint Chiefs in a purely military judgment on the question of removing General MacArthur. Of course, whether any such judgment could be purely military is another matter.

On Monday morning, April 9, General Bradley informed the President that in the unanimous opinion of the Joint Chiefs General MacArthur should be recalled. Marshall, Harriman, and Acheson all agreed with this conclusion. Thereupon Mr. Truman told the conference that he had already made up his mind to relieve General MacArthur from duty in the Far East shortly after the statement made by the General on March 24. It was decided that the remarkably successful Eighth Army Commander, General Matthew Ridgway, should replace MacArthur in all of his commands. Secretary of the Army Frank Pace, then in Korea, was personally designated to inform MacArthur of his replacement.[43]

Unfortunately for Administration plans, on the next day, April 10, rumors that the *Chicago Tribune* had heard of the Administration decision precipitated a hastening of the delicate procedure of recalling MacArthur. It may be recalled that the *Chicago Tribune*, as the oracle of Midwestern isolationism, had published the basic war plan of the Roosevelt Administration, Rainbow 5, three days before Pearl Harbor.[44] Consequently even the small courtesy of a personal delivery of the news of his relief from Secretary Pace was to be denied the Supreme Commander in Tokyo.

The frantic anxiety of the Administration to act before public opinion could, in its turn, react, would demand the last ounce of humiliation from the proud American proconsul in Asia. Without much doubt, as General Bradley was to concede, MacArthur's recall 'probably could have been handled better.' [45] But, as years later, MacArthur himself would admit of Harry Truman: 'The way he kicked me out of the Army he must have thought he was a pretty good fullback.' [46] Indeed there was a certain rough justice in the interruption of the General's luncheon with Senator Warren Magnuson on April 11, when an aide informed him of the public radio announcement of his relief.[47] In his day and in his own way, Douglas MacArthur had spoiled a good many repasts for others.

IX

The Insubordinate?

'So long as I hold my present position, I do not believe I have the right to criticize the policy or orders of those above me, or give utterance to views of my own, except to the authorities in Washington.' [1]

—Gen. U. S. Grant in 1864

'The national strategy of any war—that is, the selection of national objectives and the determination of the general means and methods to be applied in attaining them, as well as the development of the broad policies applicable to the prosecution of war—are decisions that must be made by the head of State acting in conformity with the expressed will of Congress. ... The issues involved were so far-reaching in their effects and so vital to the life of the Nation, that this phase of coordinating Army and Navy effort could not be delegated by the Commander in Chief to any subordinate authority. Any such attempt would not constitute delegation, but rather abdication.' [2]

—Douglas MacArthur in 1932

'... I find in existence a new and heretofore unknown and dangerous concept, that the members of our armed forces owe primary allegiance and loyalty to those who temporarily exercise the authority of the executive branch of the government, rather than to the country and its Constitution, which they are sworn to defend.

'No proposition could be more dangerous. ...

'Yet so inordinate has been the application of executive power that members of the armed services have been subjected to the most arbitrary and ruthless treatment for daring to speak the truth in accordance with conviction and conscience.' [3]

—Douglas MacArthur, July 25, 1951

'There was no more reason for replacing [General Joseph] Stilwell than there would be for replacing me.' [4]

—Douglas MacArthur in 1944

ON THE SAME DAY THAT REPRESENTATIVE
Martin released MacArthur's thunderbolt on the floor of
Congress, April 5, the General had answered an inquiry by
The Freeman magazine, a conservative Republican publi-
cation. In his reply MacArthur said that the reason for not
arming more South Koreans was to be found in 'basic
political decisions beyond my authority.' Since MacArthur
had himself recommended against arming more South
Koreans in January in favor of building up the Japanese
National Police Reserve, General Bradley's conclusion that
MacArthur was engaging here in an unnecessary 'implied'
public criticism of the Administration seems valid.[5] Like
President Truman, the Chairman of the Joint Chiefs of
Staff considered MacArthur insubordinate. From early
April Bradley had believed that MacArthur would have
to be relieved.[6]

General Bradley doubted, however, that MacArthur was
'intentionally' insubordinate, although he felt that the Far
Eastern Commander had no right to carry his differences
to the people while still on active duty. For himself Bradley said that he would have resigned without comment if
he had found his advice unacceptable. The Chairman of
the Joint Chiefs emphasized that the President has the
legal right to dismiss any officer from his command 'at any
time he sees fit,' even if it was simply a matter of losing
confidence in that officer's judgment.[7] Otherwise, obviously,
neither civilian authority nor military discipline could be
maintained.

General Bradley's immediate civilian superior, Secretary
of Defense George Marshall, was in agreement with Brad-

ley on the question of public debates between officers on active service and their superiors. Marshall said that, while it was 'completely understandable and, in fact, at times commendable' that theater commanders have their own ideas on how to conduct the war, what 'brought about the necessity for General MacArthur's removal' was 'the wholly unprecedented situation of a local theater commander publicly expressing his displeasure at and his disagreement with the foreign and military policy of the United States.' Marshall thought that MacArthur was so out of sympathy with official policies that 'there was no . . . recourse but to relieve him.'[8] It is notable that the Secretary of Defense had avoided committing himself on whether General Mac-Arthur was actually insubordinate.[9] Certainly in the late spring of 1951 no high official of the Administration wanted another Billy Mitchell court-martial on his hands—Mac-Arthur was enough of a popular martyr already.

From his own extensive military experience Marshall went on to recall his 'very difficult scenes' with his civilian superior in the Second World War, Franklin Delano Roosevelt. With perceptible pride the former Army Chief of Staff added: 'But I didn't make any public speeches.' Even more pointedly Marshall observed that General Eisenhower had been restrained during the Second World War, 'but there was no repercussion resulting from that.'[10] Of course, like Marshall, Eisenhower was no more than a field grade officer, while Douglas MacArthur had already become Chief of Staff during the administration of President Hoover. Upon being informed of MacArthur's relief, Eisenhower himself said: 'When you put on a uniform there are certain inhibitions you accept.'[11]

In exalting the virtues of loyalty and obedience for the soldier, Secretary Marshall's reminiscences led him back further into American military history. In contrast to that favorite of the Republican party, Gen. Leonard Wood,[12] who had rebelled against the Democratic President, Woodrow Wilson, thereby wrecking his military career, Marshall chose Gen. John J. Pershing of A.E.F. fame. In 1916 the President had barred 'Black Jack' Pershing from employing the Mexican railroads in his futile pursuit of Pancho Villa at a time when Pershing had no motor vehicles. Finally, when in spite of all difficulties Pershing thought that he had trapped Villa, Wilson ordered Pershing home, 'which meant [that] he [Pershing] had failed in his business.' After receiving this Presidential order, Pershing walked around his tent all night, but he remained silent. Concluded George Marshall: 'I think it was a very good model to follow in the Army.'[13]

There is no doubt that the military careers of Pershing, Marshall, and Eisenhower, like so many successful careers in other walks of life, were paved with agonized silences. Nevertheless by 1951 General MacArthur had already completed a career which included laurels enough for many lesser men—short of the Presidency there was really no higher post which Douglas MacArthur could achieve.

At the suggestion of Secretary of State Acheson the Joint Chiefs had been called upon by the President to give an opinion on the subject of General MacArthur's recall. If the Joint Chiefs, as a body, had not suggested MacArthur's relief of their own accord, on April 8 they had unanimously recommended it. In the first place the J.C.S. felt that MacArthur was publicly unsympathetic to U.S. government policy and it was necessary to have a commander 'more responsive to control from Washington.' A second reason adduced by the J.C.S. for MacArthur's removal involved his independent public actions, including his proposal for his own negotiations with the enemy, notwithstanding the J.C.S. directive to clear policy statements with his superiors. Nevertheless General Bradley was very careful to point out that the Joint Chiefs had never called MacArthur insubordinate.[14] Indeed, former President Truman's statement in 1959 that MacArthur never would have been relieved had the Joint Chiefs controlled U.S. policy is more than justified.[15]

MacArthur's interrogator on the Inchon landings, the Army Chief of Staff, Gen. J. Lawton Collins, subscribed to the official J.C.S. reasons for removing the Far East Commander. As an illustration of reprehensible behavior Collins pointed to MacArthur's reference to Formosa in his letter to Martin, despite his directive of December 6. In addition, MacArthur's attempt to saddle the Administration with the blame for not arming the South Koreans further had disturbed General Collins. At the same time, with obvious relief the Army Chief agreed with Senator J. William Fulbright's definition of his position. The Democratic Senator had described MacArthur's attitude as 'less than outright insubordination, but . . . still quite intolerable from the point of view of efficient and effective cooperation in a campaign.' [16]

In sharp contrast to Collins, the Chief of Naval Operations, Adm. Forrest Sherman, stressed that he was 'very fond of MacArthur.' Sherman had hesitated before recommending the General's relief; at first he wanted Secretary Marshall to talk the situation over with MacArthur privately. Sherman evidently based his final recommendation against MacArthur on the latter's lack of sympathy with the Administration. Yet it seemed that Inchon had left MacArthur a considerable residue of good-will in the high command of the U.S. Navy.[17]

On the whole, it is easy to reach the conclusion of Senator Wayne Morse that 'one might almost think that he [MacArthur] was looked upon as a military prima donna' in his relationship to the Joint Chiefs.[18] Without doubt MacArthur was granted more leeway by the J.C.S. than went to less distinguished theater commanders. Probably Senator Fulbright summed up fairly well the immediate, if not ultimate causes of MacArthur's differences with the Joint Chiefs when, as he put it: 'On the one side [there stood] an organization with global responsibilities, on the other side a man of very strong personality who is not accustomed to taking orders.' [19]

MacArthur's headstrong personality had, of course, been no secret long before the Korean War. As an outstanding cadet at West Point, as a resourceful captain at Vera Cruz in 1914, as an exceptionally bold and youthful brigadier general in France in 1918, MacArthur had rarely hesitated to oppose higher authority for the sake of obtaining what he considered due credit for a successful operation. As Chief of Staff for a period of unusual duration during the pacifistic early 1930's, as a theater commander during the Second World War, and as de facto ruler of Japan thereafter, MacArthur had attracted controversy and violent emotions—either of affection or of aversion—wherever he went. Like his father, Gen. Arthur MacArthur before him,[20] Douglas MacArthur was equally famous for the arrogance of his demeanor and his language in a society too profoundly plebeian to bear well with either. The most remarkable of the complaints which he had directed at President Franklin Roosevelt accurately foreshadowed MacArthur's attitude toward President Truman: namely, that Roosevelt 'acted as if he were the directing head of the Army and Navy.' [21] During the Second World War, Admiral Halsey, who, as Admiral Leahy has remarked, was 'no shrinking violet himself,' nonetheless had recognized a superior talent in this direction. Halsey charged MacArthur with suffering from 'illusions [sic] of grandeur' and said that MacArthur's 'staff officers were afraid to oppose any of their General's plans whether or not they believed in them.' [22] Secretary of War Stimson's conclusion seems just here: namely, that MacArthur's brilliance was 'not always matched by his tact, but that the [U.S.] Navy's astonishing bitterness against him seemed childish.' [23] Henry Stimson always knew how to defend his Army, especially against naval buccaneers.

General MacArthur's own statements since his relief tend to reflect a similar bitterness. For example, while MacArthur testified in the Senate Hearing that, up to his meeting with President Truman on Wake Island in October 1950, he had had no complaint concerning support from the Administration; subsequent to that date, in the words of the General in 1956, 'the disease of power' coursing through the veins of Harry Truman had finally brought about his recall as 'a vengeful reprisal' for his bold stand on the Korean War.

In 1956, MacArthur also considered as contributing causes of his recall, both the 'personally hostile' attitudes of Secretary Marshall and General Bradley and the Administration's supposed desire to hush up the case of the British diplomats who deserted to Communism, Guy Burgess and Donald MacLean.[24] As far as Marshall is concerned there is some little fuel—largely engendered among MacArthur's own supporters—to sustain this charge,[25] but the real criticism of President Truman remains implicit in Secretary Marshall's revealing final conclusion that MacArthur should have been relieved long before his open defiance of civilian authority. The President, in short, had been too weak rather than too strong in exercising his authority over MacArthur.

Fortunately for the more permanent reputation of General MacArthur, such explanations of his recall can, at best, be compared to his assertion during the Senate Hearings that 'no more subordinate soldier has ever worn the American uniform' than himself.[26] Nevertheless, the fact remains that if MacArthur's ex post facto rationalizations of his recall are hardly distinguished by objectivity, on the less personal and more serious levels of his conduct of the war he had a case—a case, unfortunately, which has improved concurrently with the development of the Soviet nuclear weapons program.

Total Victory

'The objective of any warring nation is victory, immediate and complete.' [1]

—Douglas MacArthur in 1931

'A democracy cannot fight a Seven Years War.' [2]

—Gen. George C. Marshall in 1949

'We do not want war any more than the West does, but we are less interested in peace than the West, and therein lies the strength of our position.' [3]

—Joseph Stalin in 1949

'Bred on imperatives, the military temperament is astonished by the number of pretenses in which the statesman has to indulge. The terrible simplicities of war are in strong contrast to the devious methods demanded by the art of government.' [4]

—Charles de Gaulle

FOLLOWING HIS ABRUPT AND GRACELESS relief, General MacArthur returned to the United States on a wave of largely spontaneous acclaim; to the chagrin of the Administration, the very model of a conquering hero rather than of a discredited general. It may now have appeared to some that what MacArthur could never realize in victory he might achieve in defeat; among unprecedented honors accorded him, the General was to address a joint meeting of Congress. This, the first of many such public forums, had been hurriedly arranged for him on the day of his recall, by House Minority Leader Martin.[5] With the ardor with which he normally pursued the enemy, Mac-Arthur had long sought for a public hearing—at last he had it with practically no restrictions on his freedom of speech or action.

In his speech to Congress on April 19, General Mac-Arthur declared that the basic new decisions in policy and strategy which he believed were required as a result of the Chinese Communist intervention had not been forthcoming from the Administration. While in his own words, 'no man in his right mind would advocate sending our Ground Forces into continental China,' the General now revealed a considerably toned down version of his program for extending the war to Red China. This program included an intensification of the existing economic blockade, the imposition of a naval blockade on Communist China, and the removal of restrictions on American air reconnaissance of nearby parts of Communist China, including Manchuria. Finally, MacArthur advocated the freeing of Chiang Kai-shek's Formosan garrison for action against the Chinese

133

mainland, with the logistic support for such action provided by the United States.[6] Since MacArthur asserted that 'in the past' agreement with his program had been 'fully shared . . . by practically every military leader concerned with the Korean campaign, including our own Joint Chiefs of Staff,' he put a good many prominent officers on the spot so far as the forthcoming Senate investigation of his relief was concerned.

In his opening comments to the Senate Committee, which met during May and June 1951 over the issues of his relief and the conduct of the Korean War, General MacArthur explained in some detail his advocacy of a blockade against and air reconnaissance over Communist China. 'I do not believe,' said the General, 'that the settlement of the Korean conflict would require any great increase in our ground forces. There is a definite limitation logistically as to what we can supply in the way of ground forces. Our great strength would be to attack basically the Chinese forces from our strength. . . . You know that the first rule in bridge is to lead from your strength. Our strength is in the air and the Navy, as compared to the Chinese. That is where we should apply the pressure. They cannot, they have nothing to resist it with. They are wide open.'[7]

Regarding blockade, General MacArthur had now reached a conclusion very gratifying to the U.S. Navy. In a statement, somewhat belatedly drawn from his own experiences in the Second World War with a widely dispersed island empire such as Japan, MacArthur said: 'There is no weapon of war, in my opinion, that is quite as efficacious as a blockade.' The General believed that the Trans-Siberian railroad, Red China's only major alternative to imports by sea, was already strained in supplying the

Soviet Far East, and thus that Soviet Russia could not spare much capacity for her Chinese ally.[8] It is possible, of course, that MacArthur may have underestimated the extent to which the civilian economy of a totalitarian society could be restricted, should the Soviet Government decide to aid Communist China seriously.

Generalissimo Chiang Kai-shek's old friend, Gen. Claire Chennault, found himself in agreement with MacArthur's view that the Chinese Communists were 'peculiarly vulnerable to the process of blockade.' Chennault assumed that the awkward possessions of the United States' NATO Allies at Hong Kong and Macao would be included in such a blockade.[9] Not surprisingly, two U.S. Navy officers, Admirals Badger and Sherman, also saw the virtues of the idea of blockading Communist China.

Offering some foundation for General MacArthur's claim of support in the J.C.S., the Chief of Naval Operations, Adm. Forrest Sherman, thought that in the event that the United States failed to defeat the Chinese Communist Army in Korea 'some other course of action would have to be taken.' Moreover, Sherman believed that it was 'very tempting to consider courses of action which are more in accordance with the traditions of a country fighting alone,' although he conceded that such courses 'would jeopardize our long-term national security on a global basis.' Sherman also supported MacArthur on another point; the U.S. Navy had plenty of ships with which to sustain a naval blockade of the Chinese Communist coast.[10]

As essential war materials, whose import could be seriously interfered with by a naval blockade, Sherman listed rubber, petroleum, chemicals, machinery, automotive and electrical equipment. Sherman said that the military sector of the Chinese Communist economy was 'largely depend-

135

ent' on foreign trade; for example, in 1951 Red China produced less than 10 per cent of her petroleum requirements, and her weak transportation system would accentuate any deficiencies. In short, concluded Sherman, Communist China would 'be forced to turn to Russia if an effective blockade were imposed, with consequent increased drain on Russian production.'

If the advantages of driving Communist China into further dependence upon Soviet supply might be open to question, like MacArthur, Admiral Sherman saw the Trans-Siberian railroad as 'the weak link' in Communist logistics. Sherman said that this famous railroad, so decisive a factor in the Russo-Japanese War of 1904-5, was 'long, inadequate and vulnerable [evidently to bombing].' However, Sherman's statistics regarding the Trans-Siberian's supposed inadequacy were not particularly reassuring; the Admiral estimated its capacity at this time as five-eighths of all Communist China's maritime imports. As a final point, Sherman admitted that the effects of economic action were slow and were not yet visible.[11]

It is obvious from the discussion before the Senate Committee that in advocating reconnaissance flights over Communist China in his speech to Congress of April 19, General MacArthur really had bombing in mind all along. Therefore, it is significant, in view of his disapproval of limitations on warfare, that the General still found euphemisms for strategic bombing necessary or desirable. Under questioning, MacArthur replied that Communist China lacked the air power to reply to any American bombing of her Manchurian sanctuary with a similar assault against the American bases in Japan. The General also doubted whether the Soviet Union was obliged to aid Communist China under the terms of her Mutual Defense Treaty of

1950 with Peiping. In fact, MacArthur believed that Chinese and Russian interests were naturally so antagonistic that he doubted whether American bombing of the jointly operated Sino-Russian Chinese Eastern Railway, which led to Russian-held Port Arthur, would precipitate a Soviet counteraction.[12]

General Chennault similarly favored bombing Manchuria, but he qualified his advocacy by suggesting that he might change his mind should the Administration offer definite evidence of a Russian intention to enter the war as a result. More interestingly, Chennault claimed that the Chinese people would favor American bombing of Manchuria, an opinion which seemed to be closer to those of the Chinese Nationalists than to that of MacArthur.[13] Rear Adm. Oscar Badger manifested more hope than Chennault of defeating the Chinese Communists in Korea, but he also wished to bomb China 'if we do not get a negotiable reaction from the Chinese Communist Government pretty soon.'[14]

Maj. Gen. Emmett O'Donnell, Chief of the Bomber Command of the U.S. Far East Air Force, likewise favored bombing Manchuria, although he was not too sure whether he was prepared for such a major operation in 1951. In November 1950, before the heavy build-up of enemy air forces following the Chinese Communist intervention, O'Donnell's chief in the Far East Air Force, Lt. Gen. George Stratemeyer, had believed that he could have 'snarled . . . completely' the Chinese air bases and supply lines in Manchuria.[15] But by the spring of 1951 O'Donnell recognized that the U.S.A.F. was inadequate for such a sustained effort in the Far East, if it were to maintain its defenses elsewhere.

On the other hand, O'Donnell felt that, since his air

force had run out of practical objectives in North Korea, only 'unworthy targets' for strategic bombing were left in that devastated territory. In any case, the U.S. Air Force had not been designed for limited war of a tactical nature, and Rosey O'Donnell was naturally even more eager to escape from large-scale land warfare than an Army general such as Douglas MacArthur. Somewhat nostalgically, O'Donnell recalled the simpler days of absolute war against Japan, when Marianas-based American bombers had seriously damaged more than fifty Japanese cities. O'Donnell hoped to do the same to China, even without the aid of atomic bombs.[16] At least General O'Donnell's testimony must have given the Chinese Communists food for thought, not to mention material ripe for their propaganda.

Notwithstanding an American bombing campaign in Manchuria, or for that matter a United States naval blockade of the Russian-held Manchurian base of Port Arthur, General MacArthur remained certain that the Soviets would not risk a global war in response. His basic theory, often reiterated, was that the Soviets would act on their own hook regardless of American actions—not a theory with much support in military history. In any event, MacArthur felt he could stop a Russian invasion of the main islands of Japan[17]—hardly an encouraging conclusion to those hostages for cautious American behavior, the almost defenseless Continental European Allies of the United States.[18]

Generals Spaatz and O'Donnell, as well as Admiral Sherman, upheld MacArthur's argument that the Soviet response to an American bombing of Manchuria would not be war. Sherman explained that in his view the 'residual power of the United States' was the deterrent which would keep the Russians from entering.[19] But, as Americans had already painfully discovered in Korea and elsewhere, there were many methods short of all-out intervention[20] by which an enemy could tie the United States down to an interminable campaign in Manchuria.

Of the final item in MacArthur's program it should be noted that the General now advocated the employment of Chiang Kai-shek's forces against only the South China coast. MacArthur, apparently, no longer favored an effort to break the hardening stalemate in Korea by an all-out assault of United Nations ground troops, reinforced with Chinese Nationalists. The General did hope, however, that Chinese Nationalist raids on the South China coast would relieve pressure on the forces in Korea; he also conceded that in 1951 the possibilities of a major Nationalist return to the Chinese mainland were 'quite limited.'[21] Wisely, MacArthur stayed out of the delicate political implications raised by the assertion of his supporter, General Chennault, that the Chinese Communists feared the activities of Chiang Kai-shek in the supposedly 'soft underbelly' of their South China coast more than those of all the remaining United Nations[22]—such Chinese Communist fears could well have resulted in the United States becoming involved in an enormous campaign of indefinite duration supporting a major Chinese Nationalist return to the mainland.

One of the most important bases for the interest of General MacArthur, as well as of the more nationalist sections of the Republican party, in a more vigorous program in the Far East, lay in the traditional American movement to the West. This deep-lying and largely unconscious force toward expansionism had affected the conservative and nationalist elements of all Occidental countries—its expression in the United States a generation earlier had brought the fathers of Douglas MacArthur and Senator Taft 8000 miles west across the Pacific to the Philippines. Although Senator Taft now led the isolationist elements of Mid-western Republicanism, however illogical in theory, in practice it was not difficult for him to rally support for any vigorous movement advocated by MacArthur so long as it was in the Pacific. Since frontier days, much like the Russian Slavophils or Prussian Junkers, the American isolationists had distrusted chiefly the sinful influence of Western Europe. Conversely, of course, the Liberal parties —in modern times in the United States, the Democratic party—included those elements which favored Western Europe and usually opposed imperial expansion in other parts of the world.

When, following his recall, General MacArthur could openly enter American political life, these ambivalent factors became quite explicit in his statements. For example, in a speech in Seattle in November 1951, MacArthur said: 'To the early pioneer the Pacific coast marked the end of his courageous westerly advance. To us it should mark but the beginning.' On the other hand, in his Boston speech in July 1951, appealing to isolationist and Irish Anglo-phobia, the General declared: 'We have been told of the war in Korea, that it is the wrong war, at the wrong time and in the wrong place. Does this mean that they [the Administration] intend and indeed plan what they would call a right war, at the right time and in a right place?' [23]

In a common link with both isolationists and nationalists General MacArthur distrusted collective security, particularly with European nations. In the Far East, on the other hand, security did not really have to be collective, since in 1951 no potential American allies there could have many pretensions toward equality with the United States in a system of mutual defense—or offense. Here, then, above all, American interests might, in MacArthur's nationalist phraseology, remain paramount, permitting the United States to go alone without the dragging effect of the United Nations or of allies who, with respect to Korea, 'do not contribute in the same generous and noble way in which we do.' [24]

With regard to the American NATO Allies, MacArthur had a further point, one of unquestioned validity so far as the smaller NATO powers were concerned. This was his appealing argument that 'if the human resources and industrial potential of the Western European nations were effectively employed for defense, there would be minimum need for American ground forces . . . air and naval power, yes, but little honest need for ground troops unless it be solely for morale purposes.' [25] Unfortunately in Western Europe, too, the conservative and nationalist elements— there so often the only groups in favor of an effective defense against Communism—preferred to put their efforts as much as possible into an already redundant sea and air strength. Among the democracies, almost everybody, it seemed, was too good for the infantry and thus for limited war.

General MacArthur thus exploited the universal dislike for ground warfare in Western nations with his popular argument that American contributions and casualties in Korea were too high. In his savage criticism of a war of containment, MacArthur asked whether the United States could indefinitely afford to 'fight in this accordion fashion —up and down—which means that your cumulative losses are going to be staggering. It isn't just dust that is settling in Korea, Senator; it is American blood.' [26]

Faced with such testimony from an erstwhile commanding general, it is not surprising that the Administration became ever more desperate to conclude the Korean War on the best terms available. It would be encouraged in this direction by Senator Knowland's cry for replacing Occidental with Asian troops in Korea, a demand which, however militarily naïve in 1951, would certainly prove effective in future American politics. Senator Harry Cain's alternative, namely the withdrawal of all American troops from Korea in the event of the continuation of the American NATO Allies' trade with Communist China, was equally well calculated to appeal to isolationist and nationalist opinion in the United States.[27]

It is interesting to compare the much bemoaned casualty rates of the Korean War at this time with those of the absolute and more popular previous war in which the United States had been engaged. By the late spring of 1951, after some ten months of conflict, known American dead, excluding missing, in Korean combat were about 13,000 men. In the three and one-half years of U.S. participation in the Second World War the number of American battle deaths amounted to about 291,000—an annual rate over five times as high as in the Korean War.[28] Even with half of the missing counted as dead, the annual death rate in Korea would be only one-fourth of that of the Second World War. Indeed, in 1942 the combat teams of one of the U.S. National Guard divisions in New Guinea had suffered a casualty rate of almost 90 per cent in a campaign, according to the official Army historian, more distinguished by MacArthur's desire for speed than by his concern on that occasion over sparing casualties.[29] From such figures, as well as from the lessons of other wars, it may well be concluded that, while any casualties at all are intolerable in an unpopular or stalemated war, any known casualties are acceptable in a popular or victorious one.

Under these circumstances one of General Willoughby's complaints takes on new light. This was his relatively natural indignation that Western Allies had put thirty-one divisions into the semi-deadlock of the Italian theater in the Second World War, when for the Korean War under similar geographic limitations they would contribute only eight. As Willoughby rightly pointed out, Italy was a strategic sideshow in World War II in which victory could not possibly be won; [30] nevertheless, in a general and unlimited war it is far easier to allocate immense resources to strategic sideshows than to obtain even minimal resources for the principal theater in a limited war. Unhappily, problems are not less real for being political rather than military in origin, whatever generals may think to the contrary.

Following his retirement, as well as before it, General MacArthur himself reflected this fundamental American faith that the great sacrifices of all-out wars were justifiable when the smaller losses of limited wars were not. Smacking distinctly of the Puritan doctrine that purgatory or limited war was an unnecessary and, indeed, immoral compromise with evil, MacArthur's ideological search for the celestial extreme of a perfect peace with no war at all or alternatively of the thoroughgoing hell of a more absolute war to realize such a peace is unusually explicit—even for an American.

Thus, in all sincerity MacArthur saw himself as absolutely opposed to war—all war. His speech to Congress expressed this: '... nothing to me is more revolting [than war]. I have long advocated its complete abolition.' [31] In his testimony before the Senate, MacArthur said: 'I am just one hundred per cent a believer against war. . . . It is a form of mutual suicide.'[32] In his speech in Boston he affirmed that Korea had again emphasized 'the utter futility of modern war—its complete failure as an arbiter of international dissensions. . . . We must finally come to realize that war is outmoded as an instrument of political policy . . .'[33]

Even before his disillusioning experiences in Korea, Mac-Arthur's role in formulating the Japanese Constitution, which forbade any military forces whatsoever, was well known, much as it may have embarrassed his supporters later on. And in commemorating the Japanese surrender in 1945, MacArthur had said: 'The utter destructiveness of war now blots out this alternative. We have had our last chance. . . . The problem basically is theological.'[34] At least today few may deny that MacArthur's attitude was basically theological.

Only a nominal contrast to the intensity of his feelings on the utter sinfulness of war appears in the General's equally vigorous repudiation of any limitations on war. As he said before the Senate Hearings: 'Either to pursue it [the war] to victory; to surrender to an enemy and end it on his terms; or what I think is the worst of all choices, to go on indefinitely and indefinitely, neither to win nor to lose, in that stalemate.'[35] If MacArthur did not favor this third alternative, neither would United States public opinion, if it were presented in such a fashion.

More specifically, in criticizing a State Department explanation concerning the Administration's desire to prevent the Korean War from spreading, General MacArthur declared that this seemed to him 'to introduce a new concept into military operations—the concept of appeasement, the concept that when you use force, you can limit that

force . . .' MacArthur continued: 'If that is the concept of
a continued and indefinite campaign in Korea, with no
definite purpose of stopping it until the enemy gets tired
or you yield to his terms, I think that introduces into the
military sphere a political control such as I have never
known in my life or have ever studied. . . . I believe . . .
if you hit soft, if you practice appeasement in the use of
force, you are doomed to disaster.' And MacArthur concluded in a classic exposition of the purely military attitude
toward war.[36] He testified: 'I do unquestionably state that
when men become locked in battle, that there should be
no artifice, under the name of politics, which should handicap your own men, decrease their chances for winning and
increase their losses.'[37]

In his speech at Boston, MacArthur went even further
in his absolutist faith against the facts of history when he
declared: 'You cannot control war; you can only abolish it.
Those who shrug this off as idealistic are the real enemies
of peace—the real warmongers.'[38] The dramatic peroration
of MacArthur's speech to Congress is probably the best
known of his many attacks on limited war. The old soldier
wound up his speech in words which may well outlive his
reputation:

> But once war is forced upon us, there is no other alterna-
> tive than to apply every available means to bring it to a swift
> end. War's very object is victory, not prolonged indecision.
> In war, indeed, there can be no substitute for victory. . . .
> Why, my soldiers asked of me, surrender military advantages
> to an enemy in the field? I could not answer.[39]

MacArthur encountered one of the first answers to this
question during the Senate Hearings when it was observed that he, too, was proposing a limited war against

Communist China, notwithstanding his desire to decrease the number of limitations upon his activities. Certainly MacArthur had violently repudiated charges that he advocated the use of any such final arbiter of battle as American infantry on the China mainland.[40] Nevertheless, the General was far from alone in his oscillations from the advocacy of a more extended war to no war at all; both prominent military and political figures—the latter, significantly, all Republicans—supported him in many of his inconsistencies.

Not surprisingly an Air Force general, Rosey O'Donnell, thought of his experiences in Korea as a 'rather bizarre war ... [from which] we can learn a lot of bad habits.'[41] Among these General O'Donnell evidently included the bad habit of limited infantry war. Similarly Gen. Albert Wedemeyer, who, unlike MacArthur, had regretted sending American ground troops into Korea in the first place, now favored fighting there for 'a decisive and victorious culmination or we should get out.'[42] Wedemeyer explained: 'I don't want to fight the enemy under terms of his creation, and manpower-wise we would be at a disadvantage if we continue the type of fighting that we are engaged in now.'[43] In his explanation, at least, Wedemeyer was approaching the Joint Chiefs' position, although he did not allude to what might happen to most American allies should the United States fight only on terms of her own choosing.

Senator Cain favored a course very like that of General Wedemeyer. In April 1951 he introduced a Senate resolution declaring war on Communist China; at the same time the Senator bid for isolationist support with a proposal to remove all American troops from Korea.[44] Senator Bourke Hickenlooper found the rules of the war in Korea 'funny' in that they seemed to favor the enemy alone, and Senator

Ralph Flanders was convinced that Communist China was fighting 'an unlimited war' against the United States, while the Americans were not.[45]

The frustration and puzzlement over the Korean War revealed by the Republican Committee members during the Senate investigation were most clearly apparent in their final Minority Report. Offering the opinion that American youth, unlike that of the enemy, should not be 'expendable,' the Republican senators went on to claim that the Administration only 'offered the vague concept of limiting the war's area while permitting unlimited casualties.' The Republican minority believed that 'the immoral, un-Christian idea of killing Chinese until the Moscow puppets sue for peace is unacceptable. . . . We believe a policy of victory must be announced to the American people in order to restore unity and confidence. It is too much to expect that our people will accept a limited war.'[46] Certainly upon MacArthur's recall, if not with his prior defeat on the Yalu, the Korean War had ceased to be splendid for the Republicans, as it had long since stopped being little for the Democrats.

In 1952 John Foster Dulles would echo this jaundiced view of limited war, saying of the Democrats: 'Ours are treadmill policies which, at best, might keep us in the same place, until we drop exhausted.'[47] For the future, in Mr. Dulles's presumably candid words in 1954, a Republican Administration would 'shape our military establishment to fit . . . our policy, instead of having to try to be ready to meet the enemy's many choices.' As his colleague, Secretary of Defense Charles Wilson, is supposed to have put it: 'We cannot afford to fight limited wars. We can only afford to fight a big war, and if there is one that is the kind it will be.'[48]

147

Like its diplomatic concomitant in containment, a policy of limited war, with limited results, was then not only immoral to many Republicans, it was also unbearably exhausting—perhaps American manpower and money would be strained, as they asserted; certainly American public opinion would become impatient. A policy, if not a reality of victory, had therefore to be announced. Yet, under the current technology, even in 1951 General MacArthur had called an all-out nuclear war 'a form of mutual suicide.'[49] Apparently any form of military reality was not acceptable to much American opinion.

The answer to what actually constituted victory in Korea in General MacArthur's definition is not as obvious as might be thought. Assuming that MacArthur's program included a Chinese Communist retirement to the Yalu, what would happen then? MacArthur himself testified that he could not 'visualize an enemy who had been cleared of Korea staying in a state of belligerency,'[50] evidently because the same American attack which would bring about his retreat could be further stepped up to the point of overthrowing the Chinese Communist Government. Such an American threat, however, would almost certainly bring about a major Soviet intervention in one form or other for the sake of saving her most powerful ally from a total defeat. Finally, as the experiences of both Chiang Kai-shek and of the Japanese suggest, the complete defeat of a popular guerrilla-type military organization in a society such as China's may be almost impossible to achieve by any purely military means, let alone those of a navy or of the strategic air force.

Another point on which General MacArthur again anticipated future Republican opinion may be found in his argument that the United States had the capacity and need to

148

'defend every place' from Communism.[51] As in the Second
World War, when he had refused to subordinate his own
theater for the sake of a concentrated offensive elsewhere
—a habitual malady of theater commanders, termed by
General Marshall 'localitis'—so in 1951 General MacArthur
rejected the principle of any order of defensive priorities
for one area over another.[52] This is not startling, since in
both the Second World War and, thereafter, the Democratic Administration had placed the Far East well below
the priority of its preferred European stamping grounds.
For example, between 1948 and 1950 General Bradley, the
Chairman of the Joint Chiefs, had put South Korea seventh
on his priority list, a list on which Europe came first.[53]

MacArthur attempted to justify his argument against
defensive priorities by claiming that his enemy was Communism everywhere, including Communism within the
democratic countries of the West, a point well calculated
to gladden the hearts of his conservative and isolationist
supporters. When Democratic Senator Brien McMahon
asked him directly: 'General, where is the source and brains
of this [Communist] conspiracy?' MacArthur at first replied: 'How would I know?' Later, presumably sensing
the untenability of such a reply, in response to Senator
Fulbright, MacArthur admitted that Soviet Russia was
the 'strongest member and the strongest supporter of the
Communist doctrine.'[54] But MacArthur's stress upon the
always popular target of internal subversion would help
distract attention from the far graver and infinitely more
expensive threat afforded by the Soviet Union.

Ultimately, of course, General MacArthur's case for extending the range and intensity of the war in the Far East
rested no more on his concessions to public opinion than
did that of the Administration against such an extension.

149

Instead, in essence, MacArthur's case was based upon a reality so painful and so fundamental that the General had wisely forborne from openly employing it at the time of his recall. Fortunately for the historian, his aides and admirers, characteristically, have been less discreet.

To a large extent the disagreement between General MacArthur and the Truman Administration revolved about the question of timing rather than the means of handling Communist China. To MacArthur and his supporters time was playing in favor of the Soviet Union; hence a decisive, immediate action by the United States was essential because otherwise the Soviet increase in strength in the future, especially in atomic weapons, would expose the United States too dangerously to Russian counteraction. In short, the tragic intensity of the whole issue of MacArthur's relief was brought about by the apparent surmise [55] of the General, and certainly of his supporters, that 1951 was almost the last chance for the United States to face a showdown with the Soviet Union. Obviously the United States always could have defeated Communist China, either in Korea or out of it, and the bitterness of successive American commanders at not being permitted to do so has often masked the real issue: [56] namely, what various Americans thought, hoped, or feared the Soviet Union might do in response to a serious bid for the defeat of Red China.

By 1953, indeed, MacArthur himself would become more explicit on the issue of timing. In a letter to Senator Harry Byrd the General wrote:

> Underlying the whole problem of ammunition and supply has always been the indeterminate question as to whether or not the Soviet contemplates world military conquest. If it does, the time and place will be at its initiative and could not fail to be influenced by the fact that in the atomic area

the lead of the United States is being diminished with the passage of time. So, likewise, is the great industrial potential of the United States as compared with the Communist world. In short, it has always been my belief that any action we might take to resolve the Far Eastern problem now would not in itself be a controlling factor in the precipitation of a world conflict.... We still possess the potential to destroy Red China's flimsy industrial base and sever her tenuous supply lines from the Soviet. This would deny her the resources to support modern war and sustain large military forces in the field. This, in turn, would greatly weaken the Communist government of China and threaten the Soviet's present hold upon Asia. A warning of action of this sort provides the leverage to induce the Soviet to bring the Korean struggle to an end, without further bloodshed.[57]

If MacArthur's argument still purported to be concerned with bringing the Korean War to a victorious close, it pointed in practice toward a very probable showdown with the U.S.S.R. at a time when the United States, if not her European allies, still could have endured an all-out war; as late as 1953, American territory may not yet have been subject to major aerial devastation.

This situation was clearly understood, even in 1951, by Gen. Hoyt Vandenberg, the Air Force Chief. In his testimony before the Senate hearings at that time, Vandenberg declared that 'today the United States is relatively safe from air attack. Tomorrow, in my opinion, we will not be,' in view of the rapid growth of the Russian long-range air force and atomic stockpile. In February 1951, Secretary Acheson had reflected a similar insight, an insight perhaps obtained from U.S.A.F. sources.[58]

In 1956, although he believed that the United States would still win an all-out atomic war with the Soviet Union,

Gen. Curtis LeMay of the U.S. Strategic Air Command warned that, unlike 1951, such a war could no longer be won 'without suffering serious damage to this country.' [59] And in 1957 Soviet Defense Minister Marshal Zhukov declared: 'In organizing their military bases in Europe and other parts of the world and in supplying certain capitalist countries with atomic weapons, the American imperialists obviously calculate that in case of a war in Europe or Asia they will be able, as formerly, to sit it out over the ocean and avoid destructive and deadly blows. Such calculations are only too naïve, of course.' [60]

In short, the conclusion on the part of the Truman Administration in 1951 that time was on the American side involved the largely unconscious prior assumption that a democracy could compete in peacetime military preparations with a totalitarian society. Yet, as will be seen, prominent Administration figures would repeatedly, if reluctantly, recognize the advantages to a democracy of a limited war so far as preparing for the future was concerned.

XI

The Wrong War

'I do not believe in our taking a position anywhere unless we can make good . . . and a successful war about Manchuria would require a fleet as good as that of England, plus an Army as good as that of Germany.' [1]

—Theodore Roosevelt in 1910

'People have been accustomed to saying that the day of limited war is over. I would submit that the truth is exactly the opposite: that the day of total wars has passed, and that from now on limited military operations are the only ones that could conceivably serve any coherent purpose.' [2]

—George F. Kennan in 1954

'If you are going to go it alone in one place . . . you have to go it alone everywhere.' [3]

—Dwight D. Eisenhower in 1953

'The conditions of victory are commitment, the condition of stability is self-restraint.' [4]

—Henry A. Kissinger

PROBABLY THE BOLDEST ELEMENT IN THE program of General MacArthur involved extending the activities of American bombers to include at least the Chinese Communist bases in Manchuria, and possibly the whole of Communist China. The Chief of Staff of the U.S. Air Force, Gen. Hoyt Vandenberg, gave the Administration's final reply on this issue.

In essence Vandenberg opposed extending the air war to China on the grounds that his 'shoestring air force' would 'lose a war against any major opposition' without a build-up of another two years' duration. It is to be hoped that this estimate of the time required to build up the U.S.A.F. was unduly pessimistic, since within a few months, with the acquiescence of the Labour Government in Britain, the Administration would decide to bomb Manchurian airfields in the event of another major Chinese Communist attack. But in May 1951 the U.S. Air Force Chief maintained that it was necessary to hold intact his bombing force as 'the sole deterrent to war with the Russians today.' In agreement with his fellow Joint Chiefs, General Vandenberg asserted that he did not wish to 'peck at the periphery,' since to do an adequate job of bombing in Manchuria alone would purportedly require the entire U.S. Air Force, thus leaving the United States 'naked for several years' from normal battle attrition. In this period the Air Force Chief also saw few advantages in extending and thus dispersing his bombing capacities into Manchuria.[5]

Vandenberg's arguments must have been more convincing than many other Administration statements because a Republican Senator, Alexander Smith of New Jersey, found them strong. General MacArthur himself admitted —contrary to his claim that the United States had the strength to defend every place—that the U.S.A.F. was inadequate for the defense of both the United States and of the American ground troops in Western Europe.[6] More recent Air Force figures tend to confirm such an unguarded admission on MacArthur's part. For example, during the three years of the Korean War—without any extension to China—the U.S.A.F. lost the equivalent of 38 per cent of its original strength of June 1950; moreover, during the limited Korean War the Russians would eventually send at least 4000 fighter planes to Communist China, giving her the third largest air force in the world.[7] The actual value of this numerically formidable force was, of course, another matter.

With a smaller inclination than the Air Force Chief to emphasize the virtues of strategic bombing, Secretary of Defense Marshall and Generals Bradley and Collins all questioned the benefits of bombing so vast and amorphous a target as Communist China, particularly since the principal Communist sources of production for war matériel were not in China in any event.[8]

In their testimony the Administration High Command went on to refer somewhat obliquely to a more serious weakness in the MacArthur bombing program not alluded to by the General's advocates. This was the fact that the U.S.-protected sanctuary and main bases in Japan and Okinawa constituted decidedly more concentrated and vulnerable targets than did Manchuria, let alone China as a whole. Furthermore, the U.S. Strategic Air Command might lose control of its airfields in Europe, fields so important for a general war with the U.S.S.R., if the United

States chose to go alone in Asia without her still reluctant NATO Allies.[9] Other arguments brought up by Administration supporters included the problem of the joint Russian-Chinese Communist operation of several of the principal railroads of Manchuria and the employment of limitations in the past on American Air Force bombing, such as the political prohibitions against hitting central Rome or Paris during the Second World War.[10]

The second item in MacArthur's program, his advocacy of an American naval blockade of Communist China, met with less direct Administration opposition. Naturally the U.S. Navy was as predisposed toward a blockade as the Air Force was toward bombing; furthermore, the Navy was far better prepared to set up such a blockade, if necessary by itself alone. Nevertheless, Admiral Sherman, Chief of Naval Operations, did not favor a unilateral American naval blockade of Communist China, both because he felt this might be considered by Russia an act of war and thus 'defeat our wider purposes,' and because such an isolated American action would promote the feeling that the war with China was simply an American war. Sherman also supported Secretary Marshall's view that without Allied naval co-operation a purely American blockade would 'leak like a sieve.' Sherman thought, however, or at least said that he did, that a United Nations naval blockade would be 'the subsequent step,' since such action on the part of the United Nations would not legally constitute an act of war. On the other hand, in agreement with the Secretary of State, Marshall hoped that a purely economic blockade of Red China would render unnecessary a naval one, although he conceded that a complete naval blockade 'in time might have a very serious effect on the stability of the Chinese Communist Government.'[11]

157

Economic measures had already stopped almost all the maritime trade of Communist China, and Admiral Sherman was well satisfied with the Allied naval assistance which he had been offered. But short of a U.N. blockade, which was increasingly unlikely, the problem of how the United States alone could prevent Chinese Communist trade through such foreign-held ports as Macao, Hong Kong, or Dairen was not stressed by Administration spokesmen. Finally, apart from the unpromising vistas of conflict with present Allies and potentially active enemies offered by the issue of a unilateral American naval blockade, the Russian land route would still remain open to Red China at least as far as the Manchurian border.[12]

Though the United States Joint Chiefs might maintain that they had disagreed with MacArthur's program for the bombing and blockade of Communist China on purely military grounds,[13] no such repudiation was possible with respect to MacArthur's proposal to employ Chinese Nationalist troops against the South China coast, whatever the J.C.S. might maintain to the contrary. American policy with respect to Soviet Russia could profess a semblance of consistency and detachment in view of the general American agreement on fundamental policy toward the U.S.S.R. Regarding China, as that political innocent, Gen. Joseph Stilwell, had discovered even during the Second World War, American policy was inextricably tangled with politics, both domestic and foreign.

By 1952 the Joint Chiefs themselves would come to favor the employment of Chinese Nationalists in Korea; at that date, long after MacArthur's recall, it was not difficult for the Truman Administration to decide upon the always available alternative of still another expansion of the South Korean forces.[14] The issue in Formosa was thus never just a simple military matter of ascertaining which troops it was more efficient to use in this or that theater; it was always a matter of a political judgment regarding the ultimate ends of United States policy toward the Chinese Nationalists and Chinese Communists.

In 1951, in arguments remarkably similar to those employed in the United States seven years later, General Bradley testified that the Chinese Nationalists should not be allowed to commit the United States to an offensive in South China as a consequence of an attack on their part. Admiral Sherman had posed this issue in honest confusion: 'Frankly I don't know how to conduct an amphibious operation in which the [Chinese Nationalist] troops fight and [the American] ships don't.' Nor, in Bradley's view, should Generalissimo Chiang Kai-shek be allowed to dissipate again his new American equipment in weak offensive actions to the detriment of his capacity to defend Formosa. The State Department naturally feared irritating American NATO Allies who did not recognize the Chinese Nationalists. It also had in mind the increased difficulty of negotiating with the Chinese Communists which would result from an American-supported Nationalist assault in South China.[15]

American Army mistrust of the combat readiness of the Chinese Nationalists went well beyond Administration-influenced circles; in this respect MacArthur himself had not always been too flattering to the Nationalists,[16] notwithstanding his desire to employ them wherever possible. For example, Maj. Gen. David Barr of the U.S. Army, an officer with wide experience of the Chinese Nationalists, opposed their use in Korea on the grounds that they were not of much value. Barr also manifested little faith in the prospects of a Nationalist land offensive in South China.

In fact, in an interesting agreement with Admiral Badger, General Barr did not rate Formosa itself very highly as a military base for the United States, although he did not want the Chinese Communists to get hold of it.[17]

Nevertheless, as usual, such military judgments on Formosa were irrelevant. On May 18, 1951, partly because of the pressure engendered by MacArthur's relief, the State Department was forced to reiterate its recognition of the Chinese Nationalists as the only government of China. In the same speech, Assistant Secretary of State Dean Rusk took the popular political position that the Chinese Communists were merely Russian puppets,[18] puppets evidently no more capable of independent action or reaction than the true Soviet satellites of Eastern Europe.

During the Joint Chiefs' discussion of MacArthur's specific program it became abundantly apparent that the General and his critics disagreed more on their fundamental postulates than on the details of how to act in the Far East. The first and most obvious of these fundamental disagreements lay in the different geographic perspectives and emphases, differences which had already become obvious in the Second World War.

In this respect General MacArthur had grievously weakened his case when he declared that he did not 'pretend to be an authority' on 'global defense'; he asked the Senate Committee 'not to involve' him 'in anything except my own area,' i.e. the Far East. He admitted that he knew about the civilian defense of the United States 'only in a general way,'[19] but suspected that the United States was 'rather inadequately prepared' against a surprise blow or a general war. MacArthur also conceded that he knew nothing about the atomic weapons situation in the Soviet Union or of the possible consequences of a general war in

Western Europe.[20] In fact, in 1951 he had no information on Russian strength opposite Alaska; in response to a question he said that this region of Siberia, so near to Japan, was 'not my theater, Senator.'[21] And in 1948 he had informed another Congressional Committee that he was 'not in a position to render authoritative advice' on Chinese problems.[22]

If the Administration had no difficulty in showing with MacArthur's own words that his program for the Far East was derived from a completely parochial or isolated view of the Korean War, in their turn the Administration witnesses revealed rather strong reactions of their own.

Underestimating the necessities of a war-in-being as opposed to one simply in potential—unlike the essentially false analogy of the Second World War—Defense Secretary Marshall felt that the defense of Western Europe remained so important that the United States had no choice but to try to hold the line in Europe regardless of the results elsewhere. Marshall believed that MacArthur's program risked 'such terrible possible consequences' that the losses in other theaters could greatly outweigh any conceivable gains in the Far East. In a partial parallel to the thinking of MacArthur's supporters, Marshall affirmed that the Russians wanted to tie the United States down and bleed it 'white' in Korea, while concentrating themselves on the far more valuable and vulnerable European continent. In any event Marshall doubted whether MacArthur's recommendations would end the war in the Far East, since the Communists had more reserves available for this theater than did the West.[23]

Similarly, Admiral Sherman stressed that, should the United States become too concerned with the Far East, 'we would then lose our ability to hold in Western Europe, which we think in the long run is more important to us, in fact almost essential...' Sherman particularly feared the Russian production advantage over the United States in the event that they were able to occupy Western Europe's numerous shipyards. 'Whereas,' concluded Sherman, 'if we lose all the Asiatic mainland, we could still survive and build up and possibly get it back again.' [24]

General Collins, likewise, testified that 'frankly, as a military man, I don't know of anything that would delight the Kremlin more than if we were to just get involved with a large military force out in that area of the world.' With Secretary Acheson, Collins feared the loss of our NATO Allies, who were so necessary in the Administration's and, especially, in a ground officer's conception of a general war.[25]

Of course it was General Bradley, the Chairman of the Joint Chiefs of Staff, who gave the ultimate formulation of the Administration's distaste for an extension of the limited war into Asia. Like MacArthur, if they had to fight, the Administration's top command, in effect, also preferred a more conventional general war to the politically confusing peripheral campaign in which they were actually engaged. Unlike MacArthur, General Bradley's personal prestige was not committed to a victory in a given theater.

Of MacArthur's proposals Bradley declared: 'Taking on Red China is not a decisive move, does not guarantee the end of the war in Korea, and may not bring China to her knees.' Following MacArthur's advice, declared Bradley, would enable the United States 'only [to] jump from a smaller conflict to a larger deadlock at greater expense.' [26] In common with almost all American military men in 1951, Bradley still tended to speak in terms of obtaining a decision, if naturally one on a larger scale than that comprised by MacArthur's area of responsibility.

Bradley was well aware of his geographic advantage over MacArthur. As he said in his opening statement for the Joint Chiefs:

> In view of their global responsibilities and their perspective with respect to the world-wide strategic situation [the J.C.S.] are in a better position than is any single theater commander to assess the risk of a general war. Moreover, the Joint Chiefs of Staff are better able to judge our own military resources with which to meet that risk. From a global viewpoint... our military mission is to support a policy of preventing communism from gaining the man-power, the resources, the raw materials, and the industrial capacity essential to world domination. If Soviet Russia ever controls the entire Eurasian land mass, then the Soviet satellite imperialism may have the broad base upon which to build the military power to rule the world.
>
> Korea must be looked upon with [a] proper perspective. It is just one engagement, just one phase.... As long as we keep the conflict within its present scope, we are holding to a minimum the forces we must commit and tie down. The strategic alternative, enlargement of the war in Korea to include Red China, would probably delight the Kremlin more than anything else we could do. It would necessarily tie down additional forces, especially our sea power and our air power, while the Soviet Union would not be obliged to put a single man into the conflict.... The course of action often described as a 'limited war' with Red China would increase the risk we are taking by engaging too much of our power in an area that is not the critical strategic prize.
>
> Red China is not the powerful nation seeking to dominate the world. Frankly, in the opinion of the Joint Chiefs of Staff, this strategy would involve us in the wrong war, at the wrong place, at the wrong time, and with the wrong enemy.[27]

163

Bradley's subordinate conclusion that Korea, too, constituted a 'poor place to fight a war' for the United States [28] was, of course, postulated upon the theory that there was a more desirable place, not to mention a more desirable time and enemy on whom to concentrate. In practice, however, the extraordinary logistic advantages which the United States had in its nearby and protected Japanese base, as well as the vital fact that the capacity of the Korean theater—unlike that of the European—could never exceed the size of the American armed forces-in-being, may very well lead to the conclusion of General Van Fleet and other MacArthur supporters that a limited theater such as Korea was the best possible place in which the United States could hope to fight a land war.[29] Similarly, given the American superiority in sea-air power, the advantages for the United States of a peninsular war should not be underestimated. MacArthur's successor, Gen. Matthew B. Ridgway, has testified that when the Communists blundered into the Korean War, they lost from it far more than did the United States.[30] But of course, by 1951 few Americans wanted to fight a limited land war anywhere, profit or loss.

As we have already seen, the question of whether Communist China constituted the best possible enemy for the United States was bound up with the general ideological distrust of Communism everywhere which was prevalent in the Republican party. On purely strategic grounds the Administration had an overwhelming case here—only the Soviet Union could seriously harm the United States in the areas of real importance to her.

Finally, on the issue of the proper timing for a war, Bradley cautiously stated: 'There are many critics who have become impatient with this strategy [of patience] and

164

who would like to call for a showdown. From a purely
military viewpoint, this is not desirable. We are not in the
best military position to seek a showdown, even if it were
the Nation's desire to forfeit the chances for peace by pre-
cipitating a total war.' [31] With Bradley, Secretary Marshall
was well aware that the Administration's policy had 'not
always been easy or popular,' but Marshall, too, was
'quite certain' that the United States was not ready for
a two-front war in the spring of 1951.[32] And MacArthur's
most determined critic among the Joint Chiefs of Staff,
General Collins, agreed with Bradley that the United States
was buying time by means of the Korean War with which
to build up its military defenses everywhere.[33] At least,
this was a safer practice than the usual custom among
democracies of buying peace on the installment plan for
a higher price in war later on.

The dangerously articulate Secretary of State put it
even more explicitly. Mr. Acheson testified: 'The basic
premise of our foreign policy is that time is on our side,
if we make good use of it.' In 1951, under the pressure of
the Korean War, few would notice the tremendous quali-
fication at the end of Acheson's statement, particularly
since the basic, implicit assumptions of open or free societies are necessarily optimistic. With characteristic insight
the Secretary of State also grasped that the underlying
assumption of MacArthur's supporters was the opposite of
his own: namely, that time was 'not necessarily on our
side.' [34] When Senator Morse suggested that their di-
vergent attitudes toward timing might be the biggest
difference between the Administration and MacArthur,
General Bradley replied that this might be so if the United
States could not resolve the Korean War otherwise.[35]

The two members of the J.C.S. who on occasion had

showed some sympathy for MacArthur's position likewise qualified in various ways their perhaps official conclusion that time was on the side of the United States. With a most unexpected skill in dialectic, General Vandenberg of the Air Force said: 'If war were a science instead of an art, Senator Johnson, I would answer unequivocally that time is not in our favor.' [36] Admiral Sherman qualified himself more bluntly, saying: 'Definitely, in the short term, time is on our side . . .' [37] Thus the Admiral left the more important issue of the long run unsettled.

Integral to the timing argument, then, was the use to which the time so dearly purchased in Korea would be put. As long as the actual fighting continued in Korea, what both the Secretary of Defense and the Secretary of State termed the 'impetus' required for a general American rearmament persisted.[38] This impetus and its results during combat were real enough; in the ten months since the beginning of the Korean War the U.S. Army had almost tripled in size, while the American NATO Allies had increased their own military efforts by at least 50 per cent. Inside the United States it was finally possible to set up absolutely essential production facilities which otherwise would have been lacking.[39]

To be sure, Administration spokesmen had to deny the dark suspicions of American voters that it desired the extension of the Korean War in time [40] for the sake of essential rearmament, much as MacArthur himself had to disclaim that his extension of the war in space might precipitate a general war. Yet in each case the disavowed arguments constituted by far the most logical rationales for their respective proponents. In essence, and perhaps in complete pragmatic innocence, the Administration was facing and attempting to resolve in its own way Mac-Arthur's ultimate dilemma: can a democracy compete in peacetime military preparation with a totalitarian regime?

Apart from their basic disagreements over geographic emphases and timing, a differing underlying assumption between the Administration and MacArthur on what the Soviet Union might do, if confronted with the General's program, appears again and again to this day. For example, in 1956, in his memoirs, former President Truman wrote:

> If we chose to extend the war to China, we had to expect retaliation. Peiping and Moscow were allies, ideologically as well as by treaty. If we began to attack Communist China, we had to anticipate Russian intervention. . . . It was not improbable that Communist China would have moved into full-scale war after we had bombed Manchurian bases. I believed Russia would have so moved also.[41]

The Sino-Soviet Pact, negotiated in February 1950, among other clauses included the following: 'In the event of one of the High Contracting Parties being attacked by Japan or states allied with it, and thus being involved in a state of war, the other High Contracting Party will immediately render military and other assistance with all the means at its disposal.'[42] Such language both lent itself to Communist propaganda and at the same time gave either contracting party a rather broad option of opinion as to what constituted states allied to Japan. In short, as Mac-Arthur's supporters enjoyed pointing out, the Russians might not actually be obliged to enter the war unless it suited their own purposes. But, as the Administration feared, there were also many halfway houses before an all-out Soviet intervention. Such limited Soviet actions could further tie the United States down in the Far East and simultaneously weaken its alliances in Europe.

In his testimony before the Senate on an area of his special responsibility, Secretary of State Acheson questioned MacArthur's assumption that Russia would not respond to broader American actions in the Far East. He declared that this hypothesis was 'certainly not well enough grounded to justify a gamble with the essential security of our Nation.' Acheson continued, however, to uphold the official State Department line in 1951: namely, that the Soviets completely dominated both the North Koreans and the Chinese Communists.[43] Of course, here, the position of the Secretary of State may have been no more than a bluff, equally useful in domestic politics or in diplomatic negotiations with the Communists.

Secretary of Defense Marshall testified that he feared a blockade of Russian-held Dairen and the bombing of Manchuria could bring the Russians into the war as well as offend the United States Allies. Marshall alluded to the then completely exposed position of Western Europe in the face of a Russian land invasion as a basic factor affecting American policy. The Secretary of Defense also brought out that the U.S.S.R. had seriously reinforced its Far Eastern garrisons since December 1950 [44]—an ominous parallel with the Chinese Communist growth in strength in Manchuria in late 1950.

General Bradley was in essential agreement with Marshall and Acheson, confessing modestly, however, that he found it hard to figure out the Russians. Likewise, while certain that the Russians could halt the war at will, Bradley did not know what conditions would evoke the mediated peace now so obviously desired by the Administration. Bradley thought that, since the United States had not yet attacked China directly, the Sino-Soviet Pact would not necessarily apply—a reaction perhaps typical of the Administration's over-legalistic approach to the question of a Communist treaty. The only disadvantage Bradley saw for the U.S.S.R. in the Korean War was a delay in her timetable, although the Soviets were at least spared the use of their own troops in the Korean War.[45] Here again Bradley, at least in public, seems to have underestimated the military advantages accruing to any society which is forced to employ its own troops.

To the great disappointment of MacArthur and his supporters—who appear to have been particularly powerful in the U.S. Navy—all the Joint Chiefs came out against his program.[46] General Collins conceded that MacArthur's program might have ended the Korean War sooner than would that of the Administration, but the Army Chief of Staff believed that the danger of a general war implicit in MacArthur's program was the overriding consideration. Collins disagreed with MacArthur on the Soviet capacity to carry on sustained operations in the Far East,[47] a particularly weak point in MacArthur's arguments, leaving entirely aside the Soviet opportunities for retaliation in still more vulnerable areas.

In this connection General Vandenberg, the U.S. Air Force Chief, offered the opinion that, in the event of a Russian entry, the latter would probably hit at Japan by air. His subordinate, General O'Donnell, frankly regretted not having had a showdown with the Russians when the United States had air supremacy in 1945.[48] For the U.S. Air Force, at least, 1951 was not D-Day.

Admiral Sherman doubted whether the Russians also were ready for air warfare in 1951, in view of their then inadequate atomic stockpile. And Sherman offered the

169

hopeful conclusion that, if the United States grew stronger, American diplomatic pressure could then induce the Russians to call off the Korean War.[49]

Patience and forbearance might in the honest opinion of the Administration and Joint Chiefs be the only methods of working out of the Korean entanglement. Nevertheless, in the words of one unhappy Democratic Senator, such a program was decidedly lacking in political 'sex appeal' and would be 'extremely difficult to sell' to the public,[50] particularly with MacArthur and Republican Congressmen constantly stressing the cost of the war in casualties.

As we have seen, the combat casualty rate of the first ten months of the Korean War was actually only one-quarter or one-fifth that of the absolute and acceptable Second World War; moreover, it was constantly diminishing in relation to the number of Americans involved.[51] But, as the Republicans were well aware, no casualties were acceptable to the American public without some hope or illusion of victory.

Very possibly Administration estimates of the appalling Chinese Communist casualty rates were exaggerated; but the reply of Secretary Acheson to the suggestions of Republican Senator Flanders that the Red Chinese manpower reserves were inexhaustible is perfectly valid; the Chinese Communist Government would not 'pick out its army as the place to start' liquidating its problem of overpopulation.[52] And General Collins would assure another doubting Republican Senator that the Chinese Communists did not have 'endless trained manpower' to sacrifice against the now highly efficient American Army in Korea. As usual, however, the politicians scored a political point against the Army Chief of Staff, when Senator Hickenlooper pointed out to Collins that the J.C.S.'s avowed objective of simply killing Chinese Communists in Korea made for poor propaganda for the United States.[53] Collins was quite conscious that the Administration could give him few other effective propaganda lines with which to raise military and public morale; after all, what American wished to fight for such an unappetizing reality as a mediated peace?

Two other points closely related to the issue of casualties were brought out by Administration spokesmen; neither was of a nature calculated to appeal much to the United States public. The first was that American veterans of the Korean War were now rapidly being rotated home to serve as seed corn for training the whole of the U.S. Armed Services in modern combat; the second point was that the British and French already had so many men tied down in the Far East, in Malaya, and Indo-China, fighting local Communists, that they could not contribute many more men to Korea.[54] Isolationist and nationalist opinion in the United States still preferred foreign seed corn to domestic, so far as combat was concerned.

During his testimony in the course of his exploitation of the casualty issue, General MacArthur encountered a politician as tough as himself, in this case a Democratic Senator—Brien McMahon from Connecticut. McMahon had just concluded that by 1953 the United States would be so strong that the Russians would not dare attack her, when MacArthur interjected: 'And in two years what will be your casualty rate of American boys in Korea?' McMahon retorted: 'And General, I ask you what our casualty rate will be in Washington, D. C., if they [the Russians] put on an attack, an atomic attack ... to say nothing of the American boys who are going to die in the air and sea in this logistical ... support of the [Nationalist] forces into China.' [55] Senator McMahon may have been unaware that during the Second World War, in the name of sparing military casualties, the Western Allies had led the parade into the ever more facile slaughter of civilians.

President Truman, Secretary Marshall, and General Bradley might all make McMahon's point in less demagogic language; after all, fear of a general and nuclear war was practically the only popular line available to the Administration. Marshall's characteristically moderate words here have a more permanent validity, a validity which alone shows how much he had learned in his role as a diplomat since the Second World War. Marshall said:

> There can be, I think, no quick and decisive solution to the global struggle short of resorting to another world war. The cost of such a conflict is beyond calculation. It is, therefore, our policy to contain Communist aggression in different fashions in different areas without resorting to total war, if that be possible to avoid. This policy may seem costly, if maintained over a period of years, but those costs would not be comparable at all to what happens if we get involved in what you might call an atomic war.... The application of this policy has not always been easy or popular. [56]

Far, then, from being without plan or policy, as MacArthur had charged, [57] the Administration was following a consistent, if not always explicit, policy of fighting a limited war to contain Communist aggression without at the same time paying too high a price in casualties. Senator Fulbright got Secretary Marshall to deny that the Korean War was "a sort of crusade against Communism everywhere.' [58] Hence it followed that, without the ends of an absolute war, absolute or more nearly absolute means were likewise unnecessary and the war could not be completed in what MacArthur enjoyed describing as 'the normal way': [59] that is, in a complete American victory.

So far as terminology was concerned, like many Administration spokesmen, Secretary Marshall was decidedly more candid regarding the Administration's means than its ends. He characterized the Korean War 'as a limited war which I hope will remain limited.' [60] In the spring of 1951 President Truman twice described the Korean War as limited; his former Secretary of Defense, Louis Johnson, had also admitted long before MacArthur's recall: 'If Russia or China came in, we would have to pull out. Korea is no place to fight a major war.' [61] As in the rugged Italian peninsula during 1943-45, war was inherently limited in Korea through the facts of geography, logistics, and the two peninsulas' relative military unimportance.

General Bradley also agreed that the Korean War was a limited war since it was fought in a limited area. Bradley reluctantly admitted that, as limited wars so often do, the Korean War might just peter out along the 38th parallel. Under questioning by Democrats, Bradley pointed out that there were 'many variations' in terms up to unconditional surrender; the recent American success in Greece, the quasi-war with France in 1799, and the Spanish-American War were all cited as cases in point of limited wars with limited ends within the American military tradition. The less satisfying but more exact parallel with the war of 1812 was not adequately discussed,[62] since, presumably, neither the military achievements of this particular war nor the rather too blunt return under the peace terms to the status quo ante bellum could be presented to the public as much in the way of a victory. Similarly disregarded were the, perhaps, too remarkable parallels in the Mexican War between Gen. Winfield Scott's difficulties with the

Polk Administration and those of MacArthur in the Korean War.[63]

Indeed, with Secretary Acheson, Bradley maintained that 'we would consider it a victory with something less than' a free and united Korea.[64] And in language which would have pleased another advocate of strategic opportunism within a context of limited warfare, Winston Churchill, General Bradley now declared: 'Circumstances, as they develop, will determine whether or not we have to take further steps' in carrying on the Korean War.[65] Finally both Bradley and General Collins repudiated outright another tenet of the U.S. Army's absolutist military doctrine in the Second World War, when Bradley said—in full agreement with Collins—that the objectives of war were not entirely military, but 'a combination of military and political considerations.'[66] Like Marshall, Bradley had learned a lot about policy in war since 1945, when he had considered Winston Churchill's desire to seize Berlin before the Russians occupied it as bidding for a mere 'prestige objective.'[67] On a higher level Bradley was now fortunately aware that war itself is a contest in prestige, however poorly adapted its more efficient military means may be to such considerations.

Perhaps more remarkably, General Vandenberg also favored a balance of power in the Far East and opposed taking the risks implicit in completely annihilating the enemy in Korea. And Admiral Sherman thought that a limited war, even one with Russia herself, would be 'more simple' than an absolute war,[68] hardly a position open to the U.S. Air Force in 1950-51.

Vandenberg and Collins went further than Sherman in conceding that not merely were the means of the Administration limited, but that logically its ends in Korea now involved a mediated peace. It is hardly surprising that with his task so much facilitated by such unprecedented American military conclusions, Secretary of State Acheson considered himself very well satisfied with his relations with the U.S. Armed Services.[69]

Acheson had, of course, attempted to pretty up his thankless diplomatic task of achieving a mediated peace by proclaiming the Korean War 'a success' and 'a powerful victory' against aggression rather than the 'pointless and inconclusive struggle' condemned by so many Republicans. Neither argument might be the whole truth, but Acheson tried to score another point in emphasizing that MacArthur's program was not ultimately aimed at an unconditional surrender of the Chinese Communists any more than was that of the Administration.[70] Here the Secretary of State was trying to have it both ways, for if, as the Administration charged, MacArthur was risking a general war, implicit in such a risk was the hope of an absolute victory in Korea. At least it says much for the candor of Secretary Acheson that at one point in his testimony he declared that the Administration was seeking 'some sort of settlement in Korea which can be accepted on the basis of mutually known strengths.'[71] Since an essential, if often unconscious purpose, of war is to ascertain the actual strength of the belligerents, by definition any peace will reflect such a pitiless discovery in one way or another.

There was a stronger argument in favor of recognizing realistically the limits of the American achievement in Korea than simply that of honesty; in General Ridgway's words, words supposedly accepted by President Eisenhower:[72]

A drive to the line of the Yalu and the Tumen would have cleared Korea of the Chinese enemy. But he would have still been facing us in great strength beyond those rivers. The seizure of the land between the truce line and the Yalu would have merely meant the seizure of more real estate. It would have greatly shortened the enemy's supply lines by pushing him right up against his main supply bases in Manchuria. It would have greatly lengthened our own supply routes, and widened our battlefront from 110 miles to 420. Would the American people have been willing to support the great army that would have been required to hold that line? [73]

In this last query by implication Ridgway had posed a fundamental question for Americans in the middle of the twentieth century, a question only slightly less difficult to answer in practical politics than its real alternative: would Americans instead dare to ascertain mutual strengths with their enemies in nuclear warfare?

XII

Triumph and Tragedy

'We can no longer afford to act as though what is expedient is necessarily immoral and what is immoral must therefore be expedient, or we may shortly find the civilized world plunged into the agony and darkness of a new *Völkerwanderung*.' [1]

—Clark Tinch

'The objective of war was conceived to be victory, that of diplomacy, peace. Neither could reinforce the other, and each began where the other left off.' [2]

—Henry A. Kissinger

'History does not forgive us our national mistakes because they are explicable in terms of our domestic politics. . . . A nation which excuses its own failures by the sacred untouchableness of its own habits can excuse itself into complete disaster.' [3]

—George F. Kennan

'As war is no act of blind passion, but is dominated by the political object, therefore the value of that object determines the measure of the sacrifices by which it is to be purchased. This will be the case not only as regards the extent of these sacrifices, but also their duration. As soon, therefore, as the expenditure of force becomes so great that the political object is no longer equal in value, this object must be given up, and peace will be the result.' [4]

—Clausewitz

IN CONSIDERING THE FUNDAMENTAL dilemma General MacArthur faced in Korea, it may be useful to look at the problem confronting his fellow showman,[5] Winston Churchill, in two general wars. To paraphrase Clausewitz, in any conflict the military means of war must be adapted to its political ends. Since in both the First and Second World Wars the military means of Winston Churchill were inherently limited, it might be concluded that, consciously or otherwise, his political ends were similarly limited. Yet we know that in the Second World War, at least, Churchill's political ends were unlimited so far as the fate of Hitler's Germany was concerned; that is, Churchill accepted an American policy of unconditional surrender for Germany rather than the logical conclusion of his own concept of limited war, such as a mediated peace. Thus Churchill's attempt to achieve unlimited ends with limited means necessarily failed.

On the other hand, from the moment of his defeat below the Yalu, Douglas MacArthur wished to expand his means, if not to an absolutely unlimited extent, certainly far more than was acceptable to the Truman Administration. From this it may be inferred that MacArthur's ends were also less limited than those of the Administration, and, indeed, we know that this was so. Unlike the Administration, MacArthur opposed Communism everywhere rather than simply its aggressive manifestations anywhere. MacArthur's failure, therefore, resulted not from any of the many flaws in his arguments for extending the Korean War, but instead from his inability as a subordinate

179

to win the Truman Administration over to his more or less absolute ends. Hence the real bitterness of MacArthur and his supporters was naturally reserved for the immediate source of his failure, the Administration. And, as the Administration so half-heartedly admitted, its struggle with MacArthur was, in effect, over the fundamentals of policy rather than over the details of its execution.

In fact, the Truman Administration was wise to limit its debate with MacArthur as much as possible to the methods instead of the ideology of war. But, in the last analysis, although Churchill and MacArthur failed in their means, they each had the consolation of realizing splendid failures.

If, in his own words in 1945, Winston Churchill had simultaneously achieved a Triumph and a Tragedy,[6] again, as with MacArthur in Korea, each leader went down with his colors flying, his many admirers cheering, and his reputation as an authentic hero probably assured for all time. The untenability of so many of the arguments employed by each in areas outside of his direct legitimate concern— e.g. MacArthur in policy and Churchill in strategy—would remain below the waterline of public and sometimes expert observation. Their transcendent sincerity on certain fundamentals and their essential rectitude on policy toward the totalitarian societies would armor them against much criticism. But the fact remains that, however great their achievements and, on occasion, however penetrating their insights, neither leader succeeded in his ultimate aims. For the future it may not be enough to say that few authentic heroes do.

Of particular importance to Americans, it should be noted, Douglas MacArthur was popular not merely for his ends, but also in his means. So powerful was the Calvinist dislike of halfway compromises with evil that the Republican members of the Senate Committee investigating Mac-Arthur's relief were quite unable to define the purgatory of limited war or even to understand the idea very well.[7]

Perhaps it was that the American public dimly sensed that it was precisely the limitations on the Korean conflict which enabled the United States to fight this war at all. The public's subconscious conclusion, then, may have been to remove the limitations on the war in the hope that the war would end, although not necessarily in victory. Ultimately, the domestic American tradition could accept the disaster of a general war; it was only the normal reality of armed stalemate which was absolutely antipathetic to the Puritan ethos.

In this connection a thoughtful recent observation of Hanson Baldwin is worthy of note. Baldwin has written: 'The first requirement for a limited war ... is a limited, well-defined political objective attainable by limited military strength ... Such a statement is essential if a national frustration, such as that which developed during the latter stages of the Korean war, is to be avoided.'[8] But as Oskar Morgenstern has suggested,[9] a success in war comparable to that resulting from Inchon is apt to cause your political objectives to be raised commensurably. In short, the basic trouble with the proper conduct of war—of any war—is that human beings are waging it for all-too-human motives and, therefore, it is far simpler to rationalize and to limit its means than its ends. Indeed this is a basic reason that Clausewitz defined war as an aspect of man's social life.

If American civilians were inclined to oppose limited war because of their temperament and tradition, the attitude of the soldiers in the United States tended to be hostile to the Korean War on purely military grounds. In practice, like the succeeding Republican Administration, General Bradley and the Joint Chiefs of Staff opposed any kind of war as the wrong war, notwithstanding their comparatively greater readiness for the limited war which ideologically they were so reluctant to justify. In the words of that only nominal critic of the J.C.S., Gen. Albert Wedemeyer, in Korea it was the Communist enemy's 'third team opposing our first team,' an American first team which in 1951 comprised about 80 per cent of the total United States effective non-nuclear military strength.[10] Reality is usually rather humiliating when the United States has persuaded itself that it is priced out of the market of world power.

Very probably the Administration bent over a good deal further than was necessary in its endeavors to reassure its allies and avoid giving undue provocation to Soviet Russia. It did not fully understand until too late the determination of the proud and already somewhat by-passed General in Tokyo, whose 'high degree of professional ability,' in Secretary of Defense Forrestal's phrase, was 'mortgaged ... to his sensitiveness and his vanity.'[11] And in his increasingly desperate efforts to win his victory and thus his vindication, MacArthur in turn failed to understand—as so many headstrong and humiliated generals have thus failed—that any government was in far greater need of prestige than himself; the need for prestige is the lifeblood of politics, if the curse of war.

Furthermore, of MacArthur's formal case for extending the war against Communist China, only his more or less surreptitious bombing program offered much hope of quick or decisive results.[12] At the same time this particular method involved the maximum of unpleasant repercussions in Europe, in Asia, and for the principal American deterrent to the Soviet Union, its strategic air command. The petty attitude of the Administration toward Chiang Kai-shek's Formosa, if not of much military importance, simply backfired politically, as such pettiness often does.

On a more fundamental level the Administration's disinclination to fight a larger war in Asia in the name of avoiding a rather improbable general war everywhere lacked candor. Of course, here the Administration was fighting for its life against its political opponents in the Republican party, who, with equal or greater dishonesty, were simultaneously exploiting both MacArthur's desire for an extended war in Asia and the public longing for no war at all. As a direct consequence of MacArthur's recall, the Republicans in 1952 managed to reap the political benefits of each of their mutually inconsistent criticisms of the Democrats. In the furious struggle which terminated his active military career, Douglas MacArthur had, at least, greatly aided in electing another Republican general as President of the United States.

Ironically, the lack of desire or will for an absolute victory manifested by the Truman Administration had resulted in considerable measure from learning the supposed basic lesson of the Second World War too well: namely, that the strategy and other means of war must be derived from and serve the ends of policy and not vice versa. Contrary to 1942-45, the military means in the Korean conflict were so subordinated that the eventual political end of liberating North Korea expected by public opinion could not be achieved at all; much as in the war of 1812, the Administration, perforce, would return rather lamely to a policy of containment along the 38th parallel. Unlike the more felicitous denouement with Andrew Jackson, the breaking of so reluctant a champion of containment as

Korea and the Fall of MacArthur

Douglas MacArthur made the Administration's failure on the offensive all too apparent; and in any event, to public opinion, the actual containment of Communism in Korea could hardly be favorably compared with the supposed containment of Great Britain in 1812-14.

If unexpectedly President Truman showed up better than Franklin Roosevelt as a war strategist, it may well have been because of his extreme reliance throughout the Korean conflict on the advice of George Marshall. The Secretary of Defense had learned at bitter cost between 1940 and 1950 the political implications inherent in grand strategy. Of course, President Truman's comparative success as a strategist constituted his failure as a war leader, since the path of an efficient grand strategy almost never coincides with that of public opinion.

Public opinion in a democracy tends to take for granted having its own way on fundamentals and thus to be unaware of its good fortune, unless it should have to defer to the interests or power of other nations. Indeed, it is usually easier to give in to an enemy's power than an ally's interest, since the compulsion of power is immediate and absolute, whereas the danger of losing allies seems less obvious or less inescapable.

Such reactions are natural in an era of national loyalties and leave statesmen with little opportunity to appeal publicly to the coalition, as opposed to the national interest. The capacity of the Truman Administration, like that of the Roosevelt Administration before it, to transcend the national interest and to wage war within the undeniably grave limitations of coalition policy affords the most significant achievement of the United States in the Korean War. Whether in the long run this often necessary subordination of the more rapid and decisive actions open only to the national interest will pay off and thus justify the Truman Administration for all time in its great struggle with General MacArthur must be left—perhaps fortunately —for the future to determine.

Notes

PREFACE

1. Charles de Gaulle, *The Edge of the Sword* (New York, 1960), 103.
2. Elihu Root, 'A Requisite for the Success of Popular Diplomacy, *The Foreign Affairs Reader*, edited by H. F. Armstrong (New York, 1947), 3.
3. Nathan Leites, *A Study of Bolshevism* (Glencoe, Ill., 1953), 370.
4. In a letter to General Sir Claude Auchinleck which has already become a classic in civil-military relations. Maj. Gen. I. S. O. Playfair and others, *History of the Second World War, The Mediterranean and Middle East* (London, 1956), Vol. II, 245.
5. Gaetano Salvemini, *Mussolini, Diplomate* (Paris, 1932), 7 (translation).
6. Irving Kristol, 'The Shadow of a War,' *The Reporter* (New York, February 5, 1959), 41-2; cf. John W. Spanier, *The Truman-MacArthur Controversy and the Korean War* (Cambridge, 1959), 10-11.

CHAPTER I. THE ANTICIPATIONS

1. Lynn Montross and Capt. Nicholas Canzona, *United States Marine Operations in Korea*, Vol. III, *The Chosin Reservoir Campaign*, Historical Branch, U.S. Marine Corps HQ. (Washington, 1957), 83.
2. Mark Watson, *United States Army in World War II, The War Department, Chief of Staff: Prewar Plans and Preparations*, Historical Division, Dept. of the Army (Washington, 1950), 18.
3. *The War Reports of Generals of the Army George C. Marshall, H. H. Arnold and Fleet Admiral Ernest J. King* (Philadelphia, 1947), 299.
4. *Time* (New York, August 28, 1950), 14.
5. *Memoirs* by Harry S. Truman, Vol. I, *Year of Decisions* (New York, 1955), 432-4, 444-5; Martin Lichterman, *To the Yalu and Back*. Ms. study for the Twentieth Century Fund under Harold Stein (Princeton, undated), 2-3 (hereafter cited as Lichterman Ms.); *Hearings before the House Committee on Foreign Affairs*, 81st Congress, 1st Session (Washington, 1949), 121-40, and *Aid to Korea Report #962*, 7-8.

6. Cmdr. M. C. Cagle and Cmdr. F. A. Manson, *The Sea War in Korea* (Annapolis, 1957), 7; 'Military Situation in the Far East,' *Joint Senate Committee on Armed Services and Foreign Relations Hearings*, 82nd Congress, 1st Session (Washington, 1951), 2415 (cited hereafter as *Hearings*); *Memoirs* by Harry S. Truman, Vol. II, *Years of Trial and Hope* (New York, 1956), 317; Gen. Albert C. Wedemeyer, *Wedemeyer Reports!* (New York, 1948), 348; John P. Sutherland, 'The Story General Marshall Told Me,' *U.S. News and World Report* (Washington, November 2, 1959), 55. In this period Wedemeyer and U.S. Joint Chiefs of Staff were even considering the employment ·of Chinese Nationalist troops as a high priority project to keep the Russians out of Pusan. Charles Romanus and Riley Sunderland, *U.S. Army in World War II. China-India-Burma Theater, Time Runs Out*. Office of the Chief of Military History, Dept. of the Army (Washington, 1959), 391.

7. *The Entry of the Soviet Union into the War Against Japan, Military Plans, 1941-1945*, Dept. of Defense Monograph (Washington, September 1955), 50-51. Notwithstanding subsequent denials on MacArthur's part. See, especially, the useful bibliography on this subject compiled by Louis Morton, 'Historia Mentem Armet,' *World Politics* (Princeton, January 1960), 161, n 4.

8. Sir Arthur Bryant, *Triumph in the West 1943-1946, Based on the Diaries and Notes of Field Marshal The Viscount Alanbrooke* (London, 1959), 508-11.

9. Lichterman Ms., 2-3, 121-40.

10. *The Forrestal Diaries*, edited by Walter Millis and E. S. Duffield (New York, 1951), 273; Carl Berger, *The Korean Knot, A Military-Political History* (Philadelphia, 1957), 89.

11. (MacArthur) *Hearings*, 382.

12. Forrestal, op. cit. 321-2.

13. *Hearings*, 2008-9.

14. *Hearings*, 1988-90. It was this famous report which Admiral Hillenkoetter of the Central Intelligence Agency would later deny having seen. 'Interlocking Subversion in Government Departments,' *Hearings before the Senate Subcommittee on the Judiciary*, 83rd Congress, 2nd Session (Washington, 1952), 7ff. (MacArthur) *Hearings*, 372, 1989, 2365, 3582. Wedemeyer, op. cit. 477-8.

15. Truman, op. cit. Vol. II, 325; cf. *Hearings*, 2327. For the sake of simplicity the rank, General of the Army, will not be employed in the text.

16. *Hearings*, 2112-13.

17. *Hearings*, 2008-13; Richard Rovere and Arthur Schlesinger, Jr., *The General and The President and The Future of American Foreign Policy* (New York, 1951), 112.

18. Ibid.; cf. 'Extension in European Recovery,' *Hearings before the Senate Committee on Foreign Affairs*, 81st Congress, 2nd Session

(Washington, 1950), 392; *The New York Times* (New York, Sept. 15, 1950), 6.

19. *Hearings*, 2009-12; Montross and Canzona, *United States Marine Operations in Korea 1950-1953*, Vol. I, *The Pusan Perimeter*, Historical Branch, U.S. Marine Corps HQ. (Washington, 1954), 33-4; *United States News and World Report* (Washington, February 17, 1956), 48.

20. Robert T. Oliver, *Syngman Rhee, The Man Behind the Myth* (New York, 1954), 295-6.

21. Truman, op. cit. Vol. II, 329; in 1952, and again in 1956, General MacArthur seriously qualified what may have been a rather nominal concurrence in 1949, *Time* (New York, November 3, 1952), 22-3; *United States News and World Report* (Washington, Feb. 17, 1956), 48; Spanier, op. cit. 17.

22. *Hearings*, 242-3, 2008-11.

23. *Time* (New York, Nov. 3, 1952), 21-2; 'Extension on European Recovery,' *Senate Hearings*, 357-65. In March 1950, Eisenhower, himself, justified defense economies on the ground that war was not 'imminent.' *Hearings before the Senate Subcommittee on Appropriations*, 81st Congress, 2nd Session (Washington, 1950), 684.

24. 'Aid to Korea,' *Hearings*, 37-43, 137-86; (MacArthur) *Hearings*, 242-3; *The New York Times* (New York, Sept. 1, 1950), 3.

25. Hanson W. Baldwin, *The New York Times* (New York, October 31, 1950), 4; and (April 17, 1959), 1-2.

26. The more rapid diminution of U.S. Army strength in comparison with the USAF in 1948-49, may have reflected the de facto Administration decision against dependence upon limited war. Gen. Maxwell Taylor, *The Uncertain Trumpet* (New York, 1960), 13-14; Walter Millis with Harvey Mansfield and Harold Stein, *Arms and the State, Civil-Military Elements in National Policy* (New York, 1958), 242-3 (cited hereafter as Millis). Forrestal, op. cit. 377.

27. Maj. Gen. Charles Willoughby and John Chamberlain, *MacArthur 1941-1951* (New York, 1954), 355; cf. *United States News and World Report* (Washington, February 17, 1956), 48; Montross and Canzona, op. cit. Vol. I, 33.

28. *Hearings*, 37-8, 229-30, 374-5.

29. *Congressional Record*, Vol. 96, Part I (Washington, January 19, 1950), 634; Berger, op. cit. 97-8; Bayley Mason, *The War in Korea, A Case Study in the Problems of Limited War*, Harvard Defense Policy Ms. (Cambridge, Mass., October 1, 1956), 15-16.

30. *Aid to Korea Report* #962, 49.

31. 'Aid to Korea' *Hearings*, 162-80.

32. (MacArthur) *Hearings*, 243, 2114-15, 3384-5, and, especially, the opening chapters of Montross and Canzona, op. cit. Vol. I.

33. *Hearings*, 948; Beverly Smith, 'Why We Went to War in Korea,' *The Saturday Evening Post* (Philadelphia, November 10, 1951), 78-80; Robert Oliver, *Why War Came to Korea* (New York, 1950), 143-8; Gen. Mark Clark, *From the Danube to the Yalu* (New York, 1954), 173-85; *The Christian Science Monitor* (Boston, June 26, 1950), 3.

34. Rovere and Schlesinger, op. cit. 99-101; *The New York Times* (New York, March 2, 1949), 22.

35. *Hearings*, 2371.

36. *Hearings*, 2664, 2678.

37. *Hearings*, 1766-71, cf. *Hearings*, 902-3.

38. *Hearings*, 902, 930-31, 1820-21, 2576-96; 'The Korean War and Related Matters,' *Report of the Subcommittee on Internal Security to the Senate Judiciary Committee*, 84th Congress, 1st Session (Washington, January 21, 1955), 19-31; Joseph W. Ballantine, *Formosa, A Problem for United States Foreign Policy* (Washington, 1952), 139-40.

39. Spanier, op. cit. 56-9; Robert A. Taft, *A Foreign Policy for Americans* (Garden City, 1951), 58.

40. *Hearings*, 1811-20; cf. *'Aid to Korea' Hearings*, 191-2.

41. *Hearings*, 3210-14.

42. *Hearings*, 2590.

43. Cagle and Manson, op. cit. 23; Raymond Aron, *The Century of Total War* (Boston, 1955), 196-8; Manson, loc. cit. 16, 30; *The Reporter* (New York, August 1, 1950), 10-11; Spanier, op. cit. 21; Taft, op. cit. 60.

44. *Hearings*, 1817-18.

45. *Hearings*, 1991-2; Willoughby, op. cit. 350ff. Montross and Canzona, op. cit. Vol. I, 17-22; *The New York Times* (New York, September 15, 1950), 6.

46. *Hearings*, 1052-3; Glenn Paige, *The United States Decision to Repel Aggression in Korea*, Foreign Policy Analysis Project Ms. (Northwestern University, August 1, 1956), Sunday, 24 (cited hereafter as Paige Ms.); Roger Hilsman, *Strategic Intelligence and National Decisions* (Glencoe, Ill., 1956), 89; H. R. Ransom, *Central Intelligence and National Security* (Cambridge, Mass., 1958), 133, 188-9.

47. *What Happened at Pearl Harbor*, Documents edited by Hans Trefousse (New York, 1958), 181, 218-19.

48. Raymond Garthoff, *Soviet Strategy in the Nuclear Age* (New York, 1958), 4; W. W. Rostow and collaborators, *The Prospects for Communist China* (New York, 1954), 67, 201; *Hearings before the Committee on Armed Services*, U.S. Senate, 82nd Congress, 2nd Session (Washington, May 21, 1952), 32-3.

49. *Hearings*, 2020.

CHAPTER II. THE CHOICE

1. Gen. Mark W. Clark, *Calculated Risk* (New York, 1950), 2.
2. Randolph Churchill, *The Rise and Fall of Sir Anthony Eden* (London, 1959), 279.
3. Dwight MacDonald, *Memoirs of a Revolutionist, Essays in Political Criticism* (New York, 1958), 70-71; cf. *Hearings before the Joint Committee on Investigation of the Pearl Harbor Attack*, 79th Congress, 1st Session (Washington, 1946), Part 20, 4013.
4. Smith, loc. cit. 80; cf. Albert Warner's 'How the Korean Decision Was Made,' *Harpers* (New York, June 1951), 101.
5. *Hearings*, 1721, 1768-9; *Truman Speaks* (New York, 1960), 25-6.
6. *Hearings*, 2574-96, 2621; Truman, op. cit. Vol. II, 334-42; Paige Ms. Sunday, 26; Smith, loc. cit. 78; Warner, loc. cit. 101-2; Rostow, op. cit. 68.
7. *Hearings*, 1110; cf. *Hearings*, 954-8, 2671-2; Alexander George, 'American Policy-Making and North Korean Aggression,' *World Politics* (Princeton, January 1955), 217-18.
8. R. E. Osgood, *Limited War, The Challenge to American Strategy* (Chicago, 1957), 166; cf. Spanier, op. cit. 18-19, 258.
9. Paige Ms. Thursday, 2.
10. *Congressional Record*, 81st Congress, 2nd Session, Vol. 96, Part 7, 9319-23; *Hearings*, 3210-17; cf. *Hearings*, 1832; Spanier, op. cit. 61-4.
11. Paige Ms. Sunday, 15; cf. ibid. Monday, 5-6, Tuesday, 7-8; Spanier, op. cit. 45-6.
12. *The Washington Post* (Washington, June 27, 1950), 4.
13. *Congressional Record*, 81st Congress, 2nd Session, Vol. 96, Part 7, 9330-35; Truman, op. cit. Vol. II, 336; Smith, loc. cit. 76; *United States News and World Report* (Washington, February 17, 1956), 50; *State Department Bulletin XXIII* (Washington, July 10, 1950), 50.
14. *Hearings*, 2585; Aron, op. cit. 179-80.
15. *Hearings*, 3210ff.
16. *Hearings*, 1651; cf. George, loc. cit. 211-15; for a different view of Sherman's position see Capt. W. Karig, Cmdr. M. C. Cagle, and Lt. Comdr. F. A. Manson, *Battle Report, The War in Korea*, prepared from official sources (New York, 1952), 6-7, 439 (cited, hereafter, as Karig).
17. Mao Tse-tung, *Imperialism and All Reactionaries Are Paper Tigers* (Peking, 1958), 29.
18. Smith, loc. cit. 88; Paige Ms. Monday, 14-17; cf. *U.S. Policy in the Korean Crisis*, Dept. of State (Washington, 1950), 63-6; Spanier, op. cit. 32-3.
19. *Hearings*, 1294; cf. Cagle and Manson, op. cit. 31; *Newsweek* (New York, December 11, 1950), 34.
20. Rovere and Schlesinger, op. cit. 104.

21. *Hearings,* 3192; Cagle and Manson, op. cit. 31ff.; Paige Ms. Sunday, 29; Karig, op. cit. 35-43; Smith, loć. cit. 78; Gen. Matthew Ridgway, *Soldier, The Memoirs of Matthew B. Ridgway,* as told to Harold Marten (New York, 1956), 192.

22. *Hearings,* 236, 536, 1112.

23. Maj. Gen. Courtney Whitney, *MacArthur, His Rendezvous with History* (New York, 1956), 332-3; cf. *Hearings,* 1012.

24. Lichterman Ms. 14; *Hearings,* 3192; Paige Ms. Thursday, 6-7, Friday, 1ff.; Rovere and Schlesinger, op. cit. 97ff.; Smith, loc. cit. 88.

25. Lt. Gen. James M. Gavin, *War and Peace in the Space Age* (New York, 1958), 122; cf. Mason, loc. cit. 28-9; John Dille's useful discussion of the difficulty of effectively employing air forces in Korea, *Substitute for Victory* (New York, 1954), 60-66, and the Special Issue of *Air Force* (Washington, March 1951), devoted to this problem.

26. Truman, op. cit. 341; *Hearings,* 3192ff.

27. Whitney, op. cit. 326. cf. Paige Ms. Wednesday, 9; Lichterman Ms., 12.

28. Truman, op. cit. Vol. II, 342-3; *Hearings,* 1084, 1129, 2621, 3382-3; Rovere and Schlesinger, op. cit. 214. For explanations of the military weakness of the Chinese Nationalists see O. E. Clubb, 'Military Debacle in Manchuria,' *The Army Quarterly* (London, January 1958), 221; F. F. Liu, *A Military History of Modern China, 1942-1949* (Princeton, 1956), Chap. XIX; *United States Relations with China, with special reference to the period 1944-1949,* U.S. State Dept. (Washington, 1949), 257, 1053. For Chiang Kai-shek's own views on the employment of Nationalist troops in Korea, see his *Soviet Russia in China* (New York, 1958), 358.

CHAPTER III. LAND WAR AND PREVENTIVE WAR

1. *MacArthur on War,* edited by Frank Waldrop (New York, 1942), 182.

2. Hanson W. Baldwin, 'The Victory at Quemoy,' *The New York Times* (New York, November 9, 1958), 4.

3. Bernard DeVoto, *The Year of Decision 1846* (Boston, 1943), 198-200.

4. *The New York Times* (New York, January 12, 1958), 44; cf. *The New York Times* (February 8, 1959), 1; (February 11, 1959), 3; (November 29, 1959), 43; Taylor, op. cit. 15-16.

5. *Hearings,* 1721; L. M. Goodrich, *Korea, A Study of U.S. Policy in the United Nations* (New York, 1956), 120-21.

6. *Hearings,* 309; American air action, however, did weaken the enemy offensive at a moment when the United States was terribly exposed so far as ground strength was concerned. Karig, op. cit. 95.

7. Whitney, op. cit. 339-40; Willoughby, op. cit. 358.

8. R. E. Dupuy and T. N. Dupuy, *Brave Men and Great Captains* (New York, 1959), 329-30; *Hearings*, 352.
9. H. A. DeWeerd, 'Lessons of the Korean War,' *The Yale Review* (New Haven, Summer 1951), 595-6.
10. Ibid.; *Hearings*, 3387.
11. Whitney, op. cit. 338-40; cf. the testimony of Gen. Maxwell Taylor, *The New York Times* (New York, March 9, 1959), 1.
12. The problem of inadequate and obsolescent equipment, again confronting the U.S. forces in Korea in 1959, of course, is endemic in a society whose conception of a 'balanced' public budget encourages the over-production of consumer goods side-by-side with a starvation diet of the most essential war matériel. Cf. *The New York Times* (New York, November 29, 1959), 43.
13. Ridgway, op. cit. 191; cf. Gavin, op. cit. 122; Eugene Kinkaid *In Every War but One* (New York, 1959), 170ff.
14. *Hearings*, 231; cf. 3386-7; Cagle and Manson, op. cit. 39-44; Truman, op. cit. Vol. II, 343-4; Maj. Gen. William Dean, *General Dean's Story*, as told to William Worden (New York, 1954), Chaps. 2-5. Pavel Monat, 'Russians in Korea,' *Life* (New York, June 27, 1960), 91.
15. Gavin, op. cit. 122-3, 173; Ridgway, op. cit. 313; Testimony of Gen. Maxwell Taylor, *The New York Times* (New York, March 31, 1959), 12.
16. *Hearings*, 232, 3381; Truman, op. cit. Vol. II, 347. Hugh Baille, *High Tension* (New York, 1959), 223.
17. Truman, op. cit. Vol. II, 345-6.
18. Truman, op. cit. Vol. II, 346.
19. Truman, op. cit. Vol. II, 349; *Hearings*, 123.
20. Truman, op. cit. Vol. II, 348; *Hearings*, 337, 369, 741-2.
21. *Hearings*, 3383; cf. 'The Korean War and Related Matters,' 16; John Gunther, *The Riddle of MacArthur* (New York, 1951), 196-7; *House of Commons Debates*, Vol. 481, 1235; Paige Ms., 17; *The Reporter* (New York, August 29, 1950), 14; Spanier, op. cit. 70-71.
22. On July 10 Prime Minister Attlee informed the House of Commons that Great Britain was not committed to the defense of Formosa. *House of Commons Debates*, Vol. 477, 957.
23. *Hearings*, 3384; MacArthur had favored supporting the Chinese Nationalists against the Communists at least since 1946. Forrestal, op. cit. 180.
24. Whitney, op. cit. 370-76 and Truman, op. cit. Vol. II, 354, give different dates for this warning.
25. Rovere and Schlesinger, op. cit. 128.
26. Truman, op. cit. Vol. II, 349-53.
27. Whitney, op. cit. 375; cf. Gunther, op. cit. 21, 196-7; Millis, op. cit. 268-70.
28. Whitney, op. cit. 377-89; cf. *Hearings*, 117, 983; R. Sherwood, *Roosevelt and Hopkins, An Intimate History* (New York, 1948), 809.

Notes

29. Whitney, op. cit. 380; cf. Truman, Vol. II, op. cit. 354-5.
30. *Hearings*, 1963-4, 2002-3.
31. Truman, op. cit. Vol. II, 354-5; Willoughby, op. cit. 420.
32. Truman, op. cit. 355-62; *Hearings*, 954, 2587, 2618-27; Johnson's relations with Secretary Acheson were strained in part over the issue of Formosa; his close and enthusiastic association with the Administrative economy drive in the Defense Department before the Korean War had also made him a political embarrassment. *United States News and World Report* (Washington, February 17, 1956), 52; *The New York Times* (New York, June 6, 1949), 1; and (September 1, 1950), 4; *Newsweek* (New York, September 11, 1950), 27-8; *Time* (New York, September 18, 1950); Millis, op. cit. 263, 280-81; Samuel Huntington, 'To Choose Peace or War,' *United States Naval Institute Proceedings* (Annapolis, April 1957), 364, N. 4; and his *The Soldier and the State* (Cambridge, 1957), 378.

CHAPTER IV. AN OPTION OF DIFFICULTIES

1. C. P. Stacey, *Quebec 1759, The Siege and The Battle* (New York, 1959), 3.
2. R. E. Dupuy and T. N. Dupuy, *Military Heritage of America* (New York, 1956), 286; cf. the same authors, *Brave Men and Great Captains*, 114-16, for the role of Gen. Winfield Scott at Vera Cruz, and Gen. George Kenney, *The MacArthur I Knew* (New York, 1951), 113.
3. 'The National Defense Program—Unification and Strategy,' *Hearings before the House Committee on Armed Services*, 81st Congress, 1st Session (Washington, 1949), 525; cf. 'National Military Appropriations Bill for 1950,' *Hearings before the Committee on Appropriations*, 81st Congress, 1st Session (Washington, 1949), 569-70; Whitney, op. cit. 343ff.
4. *The New York Times* (New York, September 6, 1950), 13.
5. Lt. Col. James F. Schnabel, 'The Inchon Landing, Perilous Gamble or Exemplary Boldness?' edited and revised by Maj. B. C. Mossman; *Army* (Washington, May 1959), 51-3; Montross and Canzona, op. cit. Vol. I, 48ff.
6. Karig, op. cit. 122ff.; cf. Montross and Canzona, op. cit. Vol. I, 58-9; Schnabel, loc. cit. 53-4; Cagle and Manson, op. cit. 86; Whitney, op. cit. 343-4; Willoughby, op. cit. 366-9; *Hearings*, 2661-2.
7. Martin Blumenson, 'General Lucas at Anzio,' *Command Decisions*, Office of the Chief of Military History, Dept. of the Army (Washington, 1959), 256; cf. Winston Churchill, *The Second World War: Vol. V, Closing the Ring* (Boston, 1951), 479ff.
8. Cagle and Manson, op. cit. 81; cf. Karig, op. cit. 161ff.; Schnabel, loc. cit. 53; Willoughby, 368-9.

9. Capt. Martin Blumenson, 'MacArthur's Divided Command,' *Army* (Washington, November 1956), 15ff., 44.
10. In recent historical interpretations, however, it was Wolfe's subordinates who pushed him into the successful final attack. But the allocation of the blame, if the assault failed, was as much to the fore in 1759 as in 1950. Stacey, op. cit. Chap. VI; Christopher Hibbert, *Wolfe at Quebec* (New York, 1959), 115-30.
11. Whitney, op. cit. 348-9.
12. Karig, op. cit. 165-9.
13. Cagle and Manson, op. cit. 76; cf. Schnabel, loc. cit. 57; *Hearings,* 1253; Gunther, op. cit. 3, 25. Cmdr. Malcolm Cagle, 'Errors of the Korean War,' *United States Naval Institute Proceedings* (Annapolis, March 1958), 34; Kenney, op. cit. 69. For the fullest account of MacArthur's talents for persuasion, see Col. R. E. Dupuy, *Men of West Point, The First 150 Years of the United States Military Academy* (New York, 1951), 383-4.
14. Cagle and Manson, op. cit. 76-8; cf. Schnabel, loc. cit. 56; *Hearings,* 1588; Karig, op. cit. 125; Henry Stimson and McGeorge Bundy, *On Active Service in Peace and War* (New York, 1947), 507; Rovere and Schlesinger, op. cit. 73; Montross and Canzona, *U.S. Marine Operations in Korea, 1950-1953* (Washington, 1955), Vol. II. *The Inchon-Seoul Operation,* 40-47; William Frye, *Marshall, Citizen Soldier* (New York, 1947), 347-64; For MacArthur's earlier, less happy relation with the Marine Corps, see Gen. Holland Smith with Percy Finch, *Coral and Brass* (New York, 1949), 19-20.
15. Montross and Canzona, op. cit. Vol. I, 3-4; Trumbull Higgins, 'East Wind Rain,' *United States Naval Institute Proceedings* (Annapolis, November 1955), 1198-1203.
16. *Hearings,* 2661-2, 2698; cf. *Hearings,* 1248; Schnabel, loc. cit. 58; Willoughby, op. cit. 374.
17. Schnabel, loc. cit. 58.
18. *Hearings,* 3431; Cagle and Manson, op. cit. 105-6; Schnabel, loc. cit. 53; Monat, loc. cit. 93.
19. 'Interlocking Subversion in Government Departments,' 2134-5.
20. Whitney, op. cit. 365-6.

CHAPTER V. THE FRONTIERS OF CONTAINMENT

1. *The New York Herald Tribune* (Paris, September 13, 1958), 3.
2. Richard L. Walker, *China Under Communism, The First Five Years* (New Haven, 1955), 272.
3. Alfred Vagts, *A History of Militarism—Romance and Realities of a Profession* (New York, 1937), 375; cf. T. Harry Williams, *Lincoln and His Generals* (New York, 1952), 133.
4. George F. Kennan, *Realities of American Foreign Policy* (Princeton, 1954), 81.

5. Maj. James F. Schnabel, 'Drive to the Yalu,' *Command Decisions* #25 (hereafter cited as 'Yalu' ms.), The Office of the Chief of Military History (Washington, undated), 21-2.

6. Oliver, *Syngman Rhee*, 306-7.

7. *Hearings* 718-19; cf. Truman, op. cit. Vol. II, 359-60; Cagle and Manson, op. cit. 112; Millis, op. cit. 274ff.; Lichterman Ms., 21-2; Montross and Canzona, op. cit. Vol. III, 5.

8. Osgood, op. cit. 201.

9. Lichterman Ms., 21-6.

10. Richard Stebbins, *The United States in World Affairs*, Council on Foreign Relations (New York, 1951), 358.

11. To be sure, neither action resulted in much political gain; in 1942, because to the great disappointment of President Roosevelt, the African landings had to be postponed until after the Congressional elections of that year. General of the Army Dwight D. Eisenhower, *Crusade in Europe* (New York, 1948), 145.

12. Osgood, op. cit. 183-4. Rather than in the narrower neckline of northern Korea.

13. Technically, the Security Council resolution of June 27, 1950, had already provided the United States with U.N. authority to cross the parallel. Lichterman, 24-6, 44.

14. Raymond Aron, *On War* (Garden City, New York, 1959), 27.

15. Much of his preliminary information from the J.C.S. of September 15 (see above) was reiterated in these formal instructions of September 27. *Hearings,* 356, 3193; Truman, op. cit. Vol. II, 360. For MacArthur's interpretation of this directive, see Montross and Canzona, op. cit. Vol. III, 6, N. 8.

16. *Hearings,* 719; Schnabel, 'Yalu' Ms. 23; Cagle and Manson, op. cit. 112-19; Whitney, op. cit. 397-8.

17. Montross and Canzona, op. cit. Vol. III, 6; cf. Whitney, op. cit. 398-9; Truman, op. cit. Vol. II, 361.

18. Goodrich, op. cit. 139; cf. K. M. Pannikar, *In Two Chinas: Memoirs of a Diplomat* (London, 1955), 107ff.; *Hearings,* 1234, 1832; Stebbins, op. cit. 359.

19. For this significant analogy, cited at the time, see *Newsweek* (New York, October 11, 1950, 23; cf. Arthur L. Grey, Jr., 'The Thirty Eighth Parallel,' *Foreign Affairs* (New York, April 1951), 485.

20. Pannikar, op. cit. 110-13.

21. MacArthur subsequently claimed that he never received this information. Montross and Canzona, op. cit. Vol. III, 7, N. 12; *Hearings,* 109, 1833; Truman, op. cit. Vol. II, 361-2; Cagle and Manson, op. cit. 116-17; Osgood, op. cit. 184; Goodrich, op. cit. 139; *Newsweek* (New York, October 11, 1950), 20.

22. *Hearings,* 758-9; S. L. A. Marshall, *The River and the Gauntlet, Defeat of the Eighth Army by the Chinese Communist Forces, November 1950, in the Battle of the Chongchon River, Korea* (New York, 1953), 7; Schnabel, 'Yalu' Ms., 3-4.

23. Baille, op. cit. 267-8.

24. *Hearings*, 2698; cf. *Hearings*, 3171.

25. Truman, op. cit. Vol. II, 362-3; cf. *Hearings*, 720, 3483-4; Schnabel, 'Yalu' Ms., 22. Spanier, op. cit. 108-12, suggests that an accidental U.S. Air Force attack October 9 on a Soviet base near Vladivostok helped to precipitate the President's decision to meet MacArthur.

26. Goodrich, op. cit. 139; cf. Stebbins, op. cit. 362; Rostow, op. cit. 69-71.

27. In 1945 General MacArthur had twice turned down invitations by President Truman to return home for a visit. Truman, op. cit. Vol. I, 520-21; *Hearings*, 433, 3486.

28. Clark Lee, *One Last Look Around* (New York, 1947), 34; cf. Whitney, op. cit. 385-7; Hunt, op. cit. 331-2; Millis, op. cit. 279-80; Robert R. Smith, 'Luzon versus Formosa,' in *Command Decisions*, 361-73.

29. Rovere and Schlesinger, op. cit. 233.

30. *Substance of Statements Made at Wake Island Conference.* Compiled by General of the Army Omar N. Bradley from notes kept by the Conferees from Washington. Prepared for the Senate Armed Services and Foreign Relations Committees (Washington, 1951), 1-6.

31. *Hearings*, 213.

32. *Wake Island Conference*, 5; Rovere and Schlesinger, op. cit. 253-62; cf. *Hearings*, 926-8, 979-80; Truman, op. cit. Vol. II, 365-7; Lichterman Ms., 45 N. 2.

33. *Wake Island Conference*, 5.

34. Montross and Canzona, op. cit. Vol. III, 36.

35. John Hersey, *Men on Bataan* (New York, 1943), Chap. 46; Samuel Eliot Morison, *History of United States Naval Operations in World War II*, Vol. I, *The Rising Sun in the Pacific; 1931-April 1942* (Boston, 1948), 151; Louis Morton, 'The Decision to Withdraw to Bataan,' *Command Decisions*, 113-23; Rovere and Schlesinger, op. cit. 46-58; Gunther, op. cit. 38-9; Sherwood, op. cit. 759; Robert Sherwood, 'The Feud Between Ike and Mac,' *Look* (Des Moines, July 1, 1952), 17; for MacArthur's version of the Wake Conference, see *United States News and World Report* (Washington, February 17, 1956), 52; Hunt, op. cit. 192-3.

36. Truman, op. cit. Vol. II, 367; *Hearings*, 41, 928; Montross and Canzona, op. cit. Vol. III, 35; Spanier, op. cit. 92-9.

37. Schnabel, 'Yalu' Ms., 4; cf. Willoughby, op. cit. 386.

38. See Seth Richardson, 'Why We Were Caught Napping at Pearl Harbor,' *The Saturday Evening Post* (Philadelphia, May 24, 1947), 80; and, especially, Brig. Gen. Thomas R. Phillips, 'The Great Guessing Game,' *The Reporter* (New York, February 18, 1960), 27-30, for the background to this old intelligence procedure debate in the U.S. Army.

Notes

CHAPTER VI. DIZZINESS FROM SUCCESS

1. *MacArthur On War*, 40
2. Mao Tse-tung, *Selected Works* (New York, 1954), Vol. II, 223-5; cf. Montross and Canzona, op. cit. Vol. III, 89ff.; Marshall, op. cit. 9; Henry A. Kissinger, *Nuclear Weapons and Foreign Policy* (New York, 1957), 344ff.; Lt. Col. Brooke Nihart, 'Mao's Strategic Defense,' Marine Corps Gazette (Quantico, Va., November 1952).
3. Capt. A. T. Mahan, *The Influence of Sea Power upon the French Revolution and Empire* (Boston, 1897), Vol. II, 392; cf. Michael Howard, 'The Armed Forces as a Political Problem,' *Soldiers and Governments, Nine Studies in Civil and Military Relations*, edited by M. Howard (London, 1957), 17.
4. Maj. Gen. George B. McClellan, *McClellan's Own Story: The War for the Union* (New York, 1887), 167.
5. Cagle and Manson, op. cit. 118-20.
6. *Hearings*, 246-7, 1249-51; Montross and Canzona, op. cit. Vol. III, 8, 11, N. 26; Willoughby, 288-90; and especially Cagle, loc. cit. 31-2; and Blumenson, loc. cit. 39-43.
7. It is regrettable that the great quantities of oral testimony readily available on this issue cannot be cited.
8. Montross and Canzona, op. cit. Vol. III, 37.
9. Schnabel, 'Yalu' Ms., 5.
10. *Hearings*, 721, 1240-41.
11. Montross and Canzona, op. cit. Vol. III, 37; cf. *Newsweek* (New York, November 13, 1950), 30-37; *Hearings, 721.*
12. *Newsweek* (New York, October 30, 1950), 30; cf. Whitney, op. cit. 400.
13. *Hearings*, 1833, 3063; Whitney, op. cit. 401-2; Lichterman Ms., 50.
14. *Hearings*, 1310, 1833; Truman, op. cit. Vol. II, 373; Whitney, op. cit. 403.
15. Schnabel, 'Yalu' Ms., 5-6; cf. Willoughby, op. cit. 386.
16. Karig, op. cit. 374; cf. Lichterman Ms., 51-4; Marshall, op. cit. 12-13; Rovere and Schlesinger, op. cit. 136; Schnabel, 'Yalu' Ms., 8; Spanier, op. cit. 114ff.
17. Montross and Canzona, op. cit. Vol. III, 98-143.
18. Richard L. Walker, *The Continuing Struggle, Communist China and the Free World* (New York, 1958), 116.
19. Schnabel, 'Yalu' Ms., 6-10.
20. Willoughby, op. cit. 393; cf. Schnabel, 'Yalu' Ms., 9-10; *Hearings*, 1833-4; Whitney, op. cit. 403-4; Truman, op. cit. Vol. II, 372-7; Lichterman Ms., 59-60; Montross and Canzona, op. cit. Vol. III, 81-2; 129-31; Spanier, op. cit. 118ff.
21. Whitney, op. cit. 405-8; cf. *Hearings*, 1833-4.
22. Whitney, op. cit. 405-8; Truman, Vol. II, 373-5.

23. MacArthur's Air Force Chief, Lt. Gen. George Stratemeyer, subsequently testified that this limited bombing was not very effective against the substantial Yalu bridges. 'Interlocking Subversion in Government Departments,' 1721. But, professedly, in late November 1950, MacArthur thought that it had been. Schnabel, 'Yalu' Ms., 22-3.

24. Truman, op. cit. Vol. II, 375-6; cf. *Hearings*, 1233-63, 1833-5; Miller, op. cit. 285-94; Schnabel, 'Yalu' Ms., 11-12.

25. Truman, op. cit. Vol. II, 377.

26. Willoughby, op. cit. 398; cf. Marshall, op. cit. 16; Lichterman Ms., 64-5; Dille, op. cit. 21; Montross and Canzona, op. cit. Vol. III, 131-3; Blumenson, loc. cit. 43.

27. Truman, op. cit. Vol. II, 377; cf. Lichterman Ms., 50; Schnabel, 'Yalu' Ms., 11-13.

28. *Hearings*, 1927-8; cf. *Hearings*, 496, 629-30, 888, 1723; Truman, op. cit. Vol. II, 377-94; Goodrich, op. cit. 150.

29. Truman, op. cit. Vol. II, 376-8; Schnabel, 'Yalu' Ms., 14-15.

30. Whitney, op. cit. 409; cf. *U.S. News and World Report* (Washington, November 2, 1959), 54.

31. Whitney, op. cit. 409-11.

32. Schnabel, 'Yalu' Ms., 13; cf. Goodrich, op. cit. 153-4; *Hearings*, 1957-9; Truman, op. cit. Vol. II, 379-80; Lichterman Ms., 63; *Newsweek* (New York, November 27, 1950), 28-30.

33. Schnabel, 'Yalu' Ms., 15-16; Lichterman Ms., 62-3; *House of Commons Debates*, Vol. 482, 1364-1459.

34. See Victor Germains's illuminating remarks on the logistics of stalemate, 'Military Lessons from Korea,' *The Contemporary Review* (London, November 1953), 266-8.

35. Truman, op. cit. 378-80; *Hearings*, 619-20; Schnabel, 'Yalu' Ms., 13-14.

36. Spanier, op. cit. 270-71.

37. Goodrich, op. cit. 154-5; cf. *Hearings*, 1734-5, 3364; *United States Policy in Korean Conflict, July 1950-February 1951*, Dept. of State (Washington, 1951), 23.

38. Lichterman Ms., 61A-2.

39. See Robert North's analyses of the motives of the Chinese Communists, including Mao Tse-tung's supposed belief in the traditional status of Korea as a frontier state tributary to China in his *Moscow and Chinese Communists* (Stanford, 1953), 272; cf. Riggs, op. cit. 279-80; Walker, op. cit. 236-7; Monat, loc. cit. 94-6.

40. *Hearings*, 1834-5; 3491-2; cf. Truman, op. cit. Vol. II, 381-2.

41. Harvey DeWeerd, *The Reporter* (New York, January 23, 1951), 26-7; Gen. R. L. Eichelberger, *Our Jungle Road to Tokyo* (New York, 1950), 181-2. For a rather blunt description in the official Australian War History of MacArthur's World War II publicity techniques, see George Odgers, *Australia in the War of 1939-1945,*

Air War Against Japan (Canberra, 1957), 97-8; or Kenney, op. cit. 240-41.

42. Montross and Canzona, op. cit. Vol. III, 142-3.
43. Schnabel, 'Yalu' Ms., 20.
44. *Hearings,* 20-21, 3197; cf. Spanier, op. cit. 124-34 and Walter Millis's unsympathetic view of this interpretation in *Arms and the State,* 296-8, and MacArthur's further justification in 1956, in which the General compared his rapid advances and retreats to those of Wellington's Peninsula Campaign. Montross and Canzona, op. cit. Vol. III, 346; N. 16.
45. *Hearings,* 1299-1369.
46. *The Reporter* (New York, November 4, 1954), 46.
47. See below, Chap. IX.
48. Willoughby, op. cit. 400-401.
49. *Life* (New York, September 5, 1955), 24.
50. Whitney, op. cit. 414; cf. Dille, op. cit. 22.
51. Whitney, op. cit. 455; *The New York Times* (New York, February 1, 1953), 7.
52. *United States News and World Report* (Washington, February 17, 1956), 51-2, 121ff.; Whitney, op. cit. 455-6; *The Reporter* (New York, November 4, 1954), 45-6; Ransom, op. cit. 173-4; Rovere, loc. cit. 26-8; Tom Driberg, *Guy Burgess, A Profile with Background* (London, 1956), 88-90.
53. Whitney, op. cit. 392; cf. *United States News and World Report* (Washington, February 17, 1956), 52; Ransom, op. cit. 89.
54. Willoughby, op. cit. 387-8.
55. *Hearings,* 123, 241-2, 350, 1035-6, 1234-5; Ransom, op. cit. 54-6, 89, 98-9, and *The Reporter* (New York, August 19, 1952), 20.
56. Schnabel, 'Yalu' Ms., 16-21.
57. *Hearings,* 123, 241-2; Truman, op. cit. Vol. II, 376, 381; cf. Gunther, op. cit. 43, and Ransom, op. cit. 66, for MacArthur's supposed discrimination against the Office of Strategic Services in the Second World War.
58. *Hearings,* 1644-5; cf. *Hearings,* 758-9, 1833-5, 2100-2101.
59. *Hearings,* 972-5, 1216-17, 1228-35; cf. Schnabel, 'Yalu' Ms., 16; Goodrich, op. cit. 151-2; Rovere and Schlesinger, op. cit. 141-2; Whitney, op. cit. 417-20; Millis, op. cit. 293-4; Lichterman Ms., 67-8.
60. Marshall, op. cit. Chap. IIff.; Cagle and Manson, op. cit. 167-9; Montross and Canzona, Vol. III, Chaps. 8-12. According to General Van Fleet's testimony, by early December the U.S. 2nd Division had lost half of its personnel and most of its equipment, 'Interlocking Subversion in Government Departments,' 2026.
61. Truman, op. cit. Vol. II, 386-7; *Hearings,* 96; Willoughby, op. cit. 398; Rovere and Schlesinger, op. cit. 143.
62. *The New York Times* (New York, November 29, 1950), 4; *Hearings,* 1834; cf. Whitney, op. cit. 421.

63. *Hearings*, 1833-5; cf. *The Pattern of Responsibility*, edited by McGeorge Bundy from the Record of Secretary of State Dean Acheson (Boston, 1952), 265.

CHAPTER VII. AN ENTIRELY NEW WAR

1. Mao Tse-tung, op. cit. Vol. I, 212.
2. McClellan, op. cit. 442. 'How many platoons in a Chinese Communist horde?' U.S. Eighth Army joke of this period in Korea.
3. Winston Churchill, *The Second World War*, Vol. IV, *The Hinge of Fate* (Boston, 1950), 404-5. A laudable principle, derived by Mr. Churchill from his unhappy experiences in 1915, but which under the terrible pressures of war, like Herbert Asquith, Mr. Churchill could not uphold in practice in 1942.
4. Mahan, op. cit. Vol. II, 156.
5. Truman, op. cit. Vol. II, 384; cf. Willoughby, op. cit. 401-2; Berger, op. cit. 126-7.
6. Truman, op. cit. Vol. II, 385-8; cf. *Hearings*, 3063-72.
7. *Hearings*, 1248; cf. *Hearings*, 652-3; Whitney, op. cit. 422-3.
8. Truman, op. cit. Vol. II, 385.
9. *Hearings*, 21
10. Cagle and Manson, op. cit. 180-81; *Hearings*, 1617.
11. *Hearings*, 972-5, 1145-6; Millis, op. cit. 295-6; Cagle and Manson, op. cit. 181.
12. Whitney, op. cit. 423-4.
13. Truman, op. cit. Vol. II, 391-3; cf. *Hearings*, 1617; Ridgway, op. cit. 193-205; Millis, op. cit. 297-9.
14. Truman, op. cit. Vol. II, 393-6; *Hearings*, 3533; cf. the page one headline in *The New York Times*, 'President Warns We Would Use Atomic Bomb If Necessary' (New York, December 1, 1950); *The Reporter* (New York, March 19, 1959), 18.
15. *The New York Times* (New York, December 5 and 6, 1950), 1.
16. *House of Commons Debates*, Vol. 481, 1166-1439, especially 1335-6; *Newsweek* (New York, December 11, 1950), 38ff.
17. Truman, op. cit. Vol. II, 410.
18. Truman, op. cit. Vol. II, 396-413; *Hearings*, 3501-4; *United States Policy in the Korean Conflict*, 26.
19. Aron, *On War*, 29; Dille, op. cit. 66-8; Germains, loc. cit. 268-9; Bernard Brodie, *Strategy in the Missile Age*, The Rand Corporation (Princeton, 1959), 319-20; *New York Herald Tribune* (Paris, June 27, 1960), 5. For an opposing view, see Oskar Morgenstern, *The Question of National Defense* (New York, 1949), 146ff.
20. As General Taylor, among others, has recently pointed out again with characteristic relish. Taylor, op. cit. 5ff.
21. *Airpower, the Decisive Weapon in Korea*, Edited by Col. J. F. Stewart (Princeton, 1957), 275.
22. *Time* (New York, February 12, 1959), 26.

23. Since interpretations of British influence on the Administration often tend to border on the conspiratorial, a relaxation of classification seems in order here.

24. '24 in G.O.P. Demand Truman Submit Attlee Pacts to Senate,' *The New York Times* (New York, December 7, 1950), 1.

25. For example such headlines as 'Attlee-Truman Discuss Disaster,' *The New York Times* (New York, December 5, 1950), 1, let alone the gross exaggerations cited in Montross and Canzona, op. cit. Vol. III, 334.

26. For MacArthur's sensitivity, see particularly Hersey, op. cit. Chap. 37, and Baille, op. cit. 216.

27. Baille, op. cit. 225-6; *United States News and World Report* (Washington, December 8, 1950), 16-22; cf. Willoughby, op. cit. 404; *Hearings*, 341-2, 3496, 3532-6; and, especially, Willoughby's blast at several prominent correspondents as 'the ragpickers of modern literature' show that animosity in MacArthur's camp over this issue had not subsided many months later. Maj. Gen. Charles Willoughby, 'The Truth about Korea,' *Cosmopolitan* (New York, December 1951), 35-7, 133-9; Whitney, op. cit. 448-9; Rovere and Schlesinger, op. cit. 11, 153.

28. *Hearings*, 3536-42; cf. *Hearings*, 1308, 3180; *House of Commons Debates*, Vol. 482, 549.

29. *Hearings*, 1630; Truman, op. cit. Vol. II, 405; 'U.S. Alerted to Red Air Raid in '50, Acheson Says,' *The Washington Post* (Washington, July 22, 1959), A14.

30. *Hearings*, 1629; cf. Truman, op. cit. Vol. II, 415.

31. Truman, op. cit. Vol. II, 415-16.

32. Truman, op. cit. 417-19; *Hearings*, 1642.

33. *Hearings*, 3504-21; Berger, op. cit. 130-31; Lynn Montross, 'Red China on the Offensive,' *Marine Corps Gazette* (Quantico, July 1953), 17.

34. Rovere and Schlesinger, op. cit. 157; cf. Dille, 22-3, for Ridgway's success as a morale builder; and Ridgway, Chap. 24.

35. *Hearings*, 2179-80; cf. *Hearings*, 2243-6; Whitney, op. cit. 429-31.

36. Spanier, op. cit. 145.

37. Whitney, op. cit. 434; cf. *Hearings*, 1465, 2180-81; Truman, op. cit. Vol. II, 433.

38. *Hearings*, 538, 3531-2; Truman, op. cit. Vol. II, 433.

39. William S. White, *The Taft Story* (New York, 1954), 161-6; cf. *The New York Times* (New York, January 3, 1951), 3, and (January 6, 1951), 4; and Taft, op. cit. 74ff. For the similar attitude of Senator Taft's father toward Korea, see W. R. Braisted, *The United States Navy in the Pacific, 1897-1909* (Austin, 1958), 181-2.

40. *Hearings*, 331-3; Truman, op. cit. Vol. II, 433-4; Whitney, op. cit. 434-5. This was more of a concession than meets the eye, since Secretary Marshall was successfully resisting pressure to

mobilize the whole National Guard. *U.S. News and World Report* (Washington, November 2, 1959), 56.

41. *Hearings*, 906-7; cf. Whitney, op. cit. 435-6; Truman, op. cit. Vol. II, 434-5; Comdr. Cagle has suggested that 'a degree of panic and inertia reigned' in MacArthur's headquarters in this period, as it certainly reigned in the field. Cagle, loc. cit. 33.

42. *Hearings*, 737-8; cf. *Hearings*, 324, 907, 1414-15, 1511-15, 1646; Spanier, op. cit. 142-4.

43. Eisenhower has observed: 'I was nine years in his [MacArthur's] office. I was a major when he was a four-star general. I was the only one who argued with him on official matters, but he kept me with him.' Sherwood, loc. cit. 17.

44. Goodrich, op. cit. 160-62; Lichterman Ms., 94-5.

45. Truman, op. cit. Vol. II, 436; *Hearings*, 503-4; cf. *Hearings*, 738-9, 1638-9; Whitney, op. cit. 437-8; Kissinger, op. cit. 50.

46. J. Miller, Jr., O. Carroll, and M. Tackley, *Korea 1951-1953*, Office of the Chief of Military History, Dept. of the Army (Washington, 1953), 9; cf. *Hearings*, 13, 47-8, 324-32, 1211, 1228; 1395-6; Whitney, op. cit. 438-9; Truman, op. cit. Vol. II, 436-7; Millis, op. cit. 313-14. General Ridgway's similar statement in December was, of course, of a strictly morale-building nature. Oliver, *Syngman Rhee*, 309.

47. Rutherford Poats, *Decision in Korea* (New York, 1954), 137; cf. Lichterman Ms., 95-6.

48. *Hearings*, 13, 48, 1277, 2956-7.

CHAPTER VIII. THE RECALL

1. McClellan, op. cit. 317.

2. Alfred Vagts, *Defense and Diplomacy, The Soldier and the Conduct of Foreign Relations* (New York, 1956), 488; cf. Williams, op. cit. 133, 350; Bruce Catton, *U. S. Grant and the American Military Tradition* (New York, 1954), 106-8.

3. H. R. Ransome, 'The Politics of Air Power—A Comparative Analysis,' *Public Policy* (Cambridge, Mass., 1958), 114-15.

4. *Truman Speaks*, 9.

5. Goodrich, op. cit. 167-8.

6. *Hearings*, 571.

7. Whitney, op. cit. 461.

8. Whitney, op. cit. 454-5.

9. 'Assignment of Ground Forces of the United States to Duty in the European Area,' *Hearings before the Senate Committee on Foreign Relations and Armed Services*, 82nd Congress, 1st Session (Washington, February 16, 1951), 6ff.; cf. Spanier, op. cit. 155ff. Sherwood has alluded to MacArthur's renewed bitterness in this period over the Democratic Administration's continued priority for Europe, as in 1942-45, under the auspices of his successful rival, General Eisenhower. Sherwood, loc. cit. 18-19.

10. *Hearings,* 3176-8.
11. James Eyre, Jr., *The Roosevelt-MacArthur Conflict* (Chambersburg, Penna., 1950), 51-6; cf. Millis, op. cit. 309ff.; Stimson, op. cit. 347-405.
12. *Hearings,* 3451; cf. *Hearings,* 3193.
13. Truman, op. cit. Vol. II, 442.
14. *Hearings,* 3450-41; cf. *Hearings,* 153.
15. Lichterman Ms., 100-101.
16. *Hearings,* 1203-4; cf. *Hearings,* 642, 920, 2948; Lichterman Ms., 96-100; William Kaufman, *Policy Objectives and Military Action in the Korean War,* The Rand Corporation (Santa Monica, June 26, 1956), 15ff.; Millis, op. cit. 315-16.
17. *Hearings,* 68.
18. *Hearings,* 1633, 2031-2; Lichterman Ms., 102-5.
19. *Hearings,* 1214-15, 3180; Truman, op. cit. Vol. II, 438-9.
20. Truman, op. cit. Vol. II, 439; *Hearings,* 346, 1213-14, 1791; Whitney, op. cit. 464.
21. Truman, op. cit. Vol. II, 443; Hunt, op. cit. 32-75, 507-9; Whitney, op. cit. 468; Kenney, op. cit. 229-30; Dupuy, op. cit. 362; Spanier, op. cit. 201-2.
22. *Hearings,* 69-72, 349; Whitney, op. cit. 467-8.
23. Truman, op. cit. Vol. II, 440-41; *Hearings,* 3181.
24. Truman, op. cit. Vol. II, 442.
25. *Hearings,* 343-4, 1775-92; Goodrich, op. cit. 170; Vagt's *Defense and Diplomacy,* 477ff.
26. Truman, op. cit. Vol. II, 443; *Hearings,* 3181-2.
27. *Hearings,* 475, 3456; cf. *Hearings,* 3195; Whitney, op. cit. 398; Hunt, op. cit. 506-7.
28. Lichterman Ms., 107-8; Berger, op. cit. 134.
29. *Hearings,* 3182; Whitney, op. cit. 463.
30. Whitney, op. cit. 463-4; *Hearings,* 1792; Millis, op. cit. 318, takes for granted that MacArthur saw the March 20 J.C.S. message on the same day.
31. *Hearings,* 3182; Truman, op. cit. Vol. II, 445-6.
32. *The Private Papers of Senator Vandenberg,* edited by Arthur Vandenberg, Jr., with J. A. Morris (Boston, 1952), 85-6.
33. *Time* (New York, February 10, 1958), 85.
34. Bryant, op. cit. 509-14.
35. Rovere and Schlesinger, op. cit. 170-73; cf. Hunt, op. cit. 507-13; Whitney, op. cit. 468.
36. *Hearings,* 446-7; cf. *Hearings,* 512-13, 1217.
37. Truman, op. cit. Vol. II, 447; cf. *Hearings,* 344-5, 1776-7.
38. *Hearings,* 1733.
39. *Hearings,* 3193-4.
40. Ibid.
41. Truman, op. cit. Vol. II, 448; *Hearings,* 372; Hunt, op. cit. 513.

42. C. Vann Woodward, *The Battle for Leyte Gulf* (New York, 1947), 29ff.; Samuel Eliot Morison, *History of United States Naval Operations in World War II*, Vol. XII, *Leyte June 1944-January 1945* (Boston, 1958), Chap. 4; *The Reporter* (New York, November 4, 1954), 4.
43. Truman, op. cit. Vol. II, 448; *Hearings*, 344-5, 739-40.
44. Capt. T. B. Kittredge, 'A Military Danger, The Revelation of Secret Strategic Plans,' *U.S. Naval Institute Proceedings* (Annapolis, July 1955); Truman, op. cit. Vol. II, 449; Hunt, op. cit. 514; *Hearings*, 344-5.
45. *Hearings*, 1096.
46. *Time* (New York, December 14, 1959), 40.
47. Rovere and Schlesinger, op. cit. 174-5; Whitney, op. cit. 470-73.

CHAPTER IX. THE INSUBORDINATE?

1. T. Harry Williams, 'The Macs and the Ikes, America's Two Military Traditions,' *American Mercury* (New York, October 1952), 38; cf. Williams, op. cit. 298.
2. *MacArthur on War*, 146-7.
3. Rovere and Schlesinger, op. cit. 315; Whitney, op. cit. 501-2.
4. Forrestal, op. cit. 18.
5. *Hearings*, 1105-6; cf. *Hearings*, 991; Truman, op. cit. Vol. II, 450.
6. Truman, op. cit. Vol. II, 442-7; *Hearings*, 1097.
7. *Hearings*, 990; cf. *Hearings*, 753.
8. *Hearings*, 324-6.
9. *Hearings*, 702; Truman, op. cit. Vol. II, 447.
10. *Hearings*, 377-90.
11. Sherwood, loc. cit. 19.
12. In May 1914, Capt. Douglas MacArthur had written General Wood suggesting that the latter would inevitably arrive some day in the White House. Walter Millis, *Arms and Men, A Study in American Military History* (New York, 1956), 214.
13. *Hearings*, 380-89.
14. *Hearings*, 878-9; cf. *Hearings*, 746, 893, 1095, 1572.
15. *Truman Speaks*, 24.
16. *Hearings*, 1253-4; cf. *Hearings*, 1187, 1199, 1208-9, 1283.
17. *Hearings*, 1537; cf. *Hearings*, 1572-99.
18. *Hearings*, 1314.
19. *Hearings*, 1146-7; cf. Forrestal, op. cit. 270; Wedemeyer, op. cit. 194.
20. Margaret Leech, *In the Days of McKinley* (New York, 1959), 572; Hersey, op. cit. 45-57.
21. Rovere and Schlesinger, op. cit. 119; cf. Hunt, op. cit. 32-83; Dupuy, op. cit. 364; and, especially, T. Harry Williams's provocative contrast between MacArthur and Eisenhower. Williams, loc. cit. 34-9, and Kenneth Davis, *Soldier of Democracy, A Biography of Dwight D. Eisenhower* (New York, 1952), 214-17.

22. Fleet Adm. William Leahy, *I Was There—The Personal Story of the Chief of Staff to Presidents Roosevelt and Truman Based on His Notes and Diaries Made at the Time* (New York, 1950), 229-309.
23. Stimson, op. cit. 507.
24. *United States News and World Report* (Washington, February 17, 1956), 51-2.
25. Richard Rovere, 'The Evil Conspiracy Against General MacArthur,' *The New Republic* (New York, April 9, 1956), 25ff.; Clark Lee and Richard Henschel, *Douglas MacArthur* (New York, 1952), 115-26; Hunt, op. cit. 42, 160-63; 313-14; Frye, op. cit. 225-7, 307-8, 364; Harvey De Weerd, *The Reporter* (New York, January 8, 1952), 18; *United States News and World Report* (Washington, November 2, 1959), 54.
26. *Hearings*, 27; cf. *Hearings*, 99, 284, 3183; Spanier, op. cit. 11.

Chapter X. Total Victory

1. *MacArthur on War*, 56.
2. Maurice Matloff, *United States Army in World War II, The War Department, Strategic Planning for Coalition Warfare 1943-1944*. Office of the Chief of Military History, Dept. of the Army (Washington, 1949), 5. See below for Marshall's shift by 1951.
3. *Time* (New York, June 13, 1949), 225; cf. Aron, *On War*, 25.
4. *The Edge of the Sword*, 106.
5. Rovere and Schlesinger, op. cit. 177-8.
6. *Hearings*, 165ff., 3553ff.
7. *Hearings*, 49.
8. *Hearings*, 179; cf. *Hearings*, 58.
9. *Hearings*, 136-7; cf. *Hearings*, 3342-9.
10. *Hearings*, 1527-33; cf. *Hearings*, 1569, 2738.
11. *Hearings*, 1512-21; cf. Bryant, op. cit. 306-7.
12. *Hearings*, 249-65; Baille, op. cit. 226-7; Rostow, op. cit. 188ff.
13. At the end of 1950 Chiang Kai-shek had doubted the benefits of atomic bombing in Manchuria, although regarding military targets he seems to have upheld Chennault's position. *United States News and World Report* (Washington, December 15, 1950), 17. In 1948 General Chennault had cast doubt on China's relative vulnerability to atomic bombing. 'United States Foreign Policy for a Post-war Recovery Program,' *Hearings before the House Committee on Foreign Affairs*, 80th Congress, 2nd Session (Washington, March 3-10, 1948), Part II, 2213.
14. *Hearings*, 2739; cf. *Hearings*, 3342-9.
15. 'Interlocking Subversion in Government Departments,' 1724-36.
16. *Hearings*, 3065-111; cf. General Spaatz's complementary dislike of infantry war, a distaste normal among Air Force generals. Baille, op. cit. 263.

17. *Hearings,* 196, 254-6.
18. In the non-public Soviet General Staff journal in June 1950, a Russian general had warned the United States about counting on the immunity of Western Europe in a general war. Raymond Garthoff, 'The Soviet Image of the Enemy,' *Military Affairs* (Washington, Winter 1957), 172.
19. *Hearings,* 1587; cf. *Hearings,* 1413, 3079-84.
20. Cf. Communist statements along this line from 1915 through 1954. Leites, op. cit. 254; Garthoff, '*Soviet Strategy in the Nuclear Age,*' 98, 113-14.
21. *Hearings,* 197; cf. *Hearings,* 265-7; *The New York Times* (New York, February 1, 1953), 7.
22. *Hearings,* 3345-6; Chiang Kai-shek, op. cit. 357-8.
23. Whitney, op. cit. 496-8; cf. Kennan, *American Diplomacy, 1900-1950* (Chicago, 1951), 53.
24. *Hearings,* 104; cf. *Hearings,* 198, 297, 3553ff.; Rovere and Schlesinger, op. cit. 221-3; Whitney, op. cit. 545-6.
25. Whitney, op. cit. 499.
26. *Hearings,* 30; cf. *Hearings,* 69. On another occasion General Willoughby has played down the casualties in Korea—here MacArthur was being blamed for them. Willoughby, loc. cit. 137-8. For a relatively objective appraisal, favorable to MacArthur on this issue, see Adm. C. Turner Joy, *How Communists Negotiate* (New York, 1955), 177.
27. *Hearings,* 1615, 2489-90, 3049.
28. *Hearings,* 219, 956-82, 3196, 3278.
29. Samuel Milner, *United States Army in World War II, The War in the Pacific, Victory in Papua,* Office of the Chief of Military History (Washington, 1957), 370-71; 'Book Review,' *United States Naval Proceedings* (Annapolis, November 1954), 1278. Normally, of course, MacArthur's Pacific campaigns resulted in a very high percentage of Japanese casualties in comparison with American, once the wretched job in Papua was completed. Cf. *The Entry of the Soviet Union into the War against Japan,* 79.
30. Willoughby, op. cit. 404.
31. *Hearings,* 3615.
32. *Hearings,* 145.
33. Rovere and Schlesinger, op. cit. 317-18.
34. *Hearings,* 3615; cf. 'Tokyo Examines Anti-War Pledge,' *The New York Times* (New York, November 23, 1957), 9; and, particularly, Robert Osgood's superb analysis of the psychology of absolutism. Osgood, op. cit. 17-33, 115; Whitney, op. cit. 541-2; Huntington, op. cit. 370-72; Hersey, op. cit. 175-6.
35. *Hearings,* 67; cf. Spanier, op. cit. 5.
36. That is, in treating war as an end in itself. Cf. Spanier, op. cit. 274-7 and Hans J. Morgenthau, *In Defense of the National Interest, A Critical Examination of American Foreign Policy* (New

York, 1951), 32. Contrast with the opposing view, as cited in Brodie, op. cit. 356, favoring limited war, a characteristic position and, perhaps, 'vice of the intellectuals.'

37. *Hearings*, 39-45; cf. Whitney, op. cit. 509, 544; Willoughby, op. cit. 416; Rovere and Schelsinger, op. cit. 225-6.

38. Rovere and Schlesinger, op. cit. 318. To show how U.S. Army opinion has changed in recent years, see particularly Gen. Maxwell Taylor's recent description of limited war as the norm of the nuclear age. Taylor cites eighteen limited engagements since 1945, 'Our Great Military Fallacy,' *Look* (Des Moines, November 24, 1959), 28, and op. cit. 5-6.

39. *Hearings*, 3615-16; cf. especially Kennan, op. cit. 101-2, and Millis, *Arms and the State*, 114, for MacArthur's similar views in 1931. See also Raymond Aron's discussion of MacArthur's concept of total victory, with its logical but often undesirable conclusion in unconditional surrender. Aron, op. cit. 29-30.

40. *Hearings*, 103, 165ff., 1019, 1946; Osgood, op. cit. 173-4.

41. *Hearings*, 3066.

42. *Hearings*, 2454-5; cf. *Hearings*, 2438.

43. *Hearings*, 2519-23.

44. *Hearings*, 2489-90, 2518.

45. *Hearings*, 1597, 1946.

46. *Hearings*, 3589-90. Medieval thought, as usual notwithstanding, dogmatically speaking it was proper for the party of Calvinist orthodoxy to regard the purgatory of limited war as un-Christian. The more heterodox Democrats would have less difficulty in this respect; cf. George F. Kennan, 'Foreign Policy and Christian Conscience,' *The Atlantic* (Boston, May 1959), 44ff.

47. 'A Policy of Boldness,' *Life* (New York, May 19, 1952), 146ff.

48. Gavin, op. cit. 124-5. For the evolution of this Republican doctrine from a British staff paper previously rejected by General Bradley, see Alastair Buchan, 'Their Bomb and Ours,' *Encounter* (London, January 1959), 16; cf. especially Bernard Brodie's burning comments on this position, 'Unlimited Weapons and Limited War,' *The Reporter* (New York, November 18, 1954), 20, and op. cit. 248-63; Henry A. Kissinger, 'Military Policy and Defense of the "Grey Areas,"' *Foreign Affairs* (New York, April 1955), 425; and Dean Acheson, *Power and Diplomacy* (Cambridge, 1958), 48-53; Gen. Maxwell Taylor, loc. cit. 30ff., and op. cit. 16ff.

49. *Hearings*, 145.

50. Rovere and Schlesinger, op. cit. 239-40.

51. *Hearings*, 83; cf. *Hearings*, 120.

52. H. A. De Weerd, 'Marshall, Organizer of Victory,' *Infantry Journal* (Washington, January 1947), 15-17.

53. *The New York Times* (Amsterdam, September 12, 1958), 3; cf., for example, the perhaps too sharp contrast made between the

outlooks of the purportedly Europe-first pragmatists and the Asia-first absolutists among top U.S. soldiers, stemming from the Second World War. Morris Janowitz, *The Professional Soldier, A Social and Political Portrait* (Glencoe, Ill., 1960), 288-301.

54. *Hearings*, 101, 299-300.
55. *Hearings*, 80, 217, 291.
56. Baille, op. cit. 226; *Hearings*, 217; 'The Korean War and Related Matters,' 6-23; Cagle and Manson, op. cit. 397; 'Interlocking Subversion in Government Departments,' 2041; Gen. Mark Clark, *From the Danube to the Yalu*, 71-82; Gen. James A. Van Fleet, 'Catastrophe in Asia,' *U.S. News and World Report* (Washington, September 14, 1954), 28; Huntington, op. cit. 390; Millis, op. cit. 330-31, 363-5; Joy, op. cit. 176.
57. Whitney, op. cit. 536-7; 'Interlocking Subversion in Government Departments,' 2034-5; cf. *Hearings*, 65-9; Hunt, op. cit. 497.
58. *Hearings*, 1379-80; 1496-8; cf. Acheson, *The Pattern of Responsibility*, 92-3.
59. *The New York Times* (New York, December 4, 1956), 14; cf. Garthoff, *Soviet Strategy in the Nuclear Age*, 156ff.; *The New York Times* (New York, May 1, 1956), 1.
60. *The New York Times* (New York, March 20, 1957), 3; cf. Garthoff, op. cit. 102-4, 110, 137-8.

CHAPTER XI. THE WRONG WAR

1. A. Whitney Griswold, *The Far Eastern Policy of the United States* (New York, 1938), 132.
2. Kennan, *Realities of American Foreign Policy*, 80.
3. Robert Donovan, *Eisenhower, the Inside Story* (New York, 1956), 137.
4. Kissinger, *A World Restored: Metternich, Castlereagh and the Problems of Peace, 1812-22* (Boston, 1957), 138.
5. *Hearings*, 1379ff.; cf. *Hearings*, 1402, 1499-1501, 1941, 3080; Dille, op. cit. 68-70; *The Memoirs of the Right Honorable Sir Anthony Eden, Full Circle* (London, 1960), 15-18.
6. *Hearings*, 287, 1393, 3094.
7. Stewart, op. cit. 287-328; cf. *Hearings*, 360, 743, 1002-3, 1588.
8. *Hearings*, 351-2, 368, 492, 617, 744, 965, 1055, 1245-6, 1402.
9. *Hearings*, 368-9, 399-402, 751, 884, 892, 1366; cf. Stewart, op. cit. 276.
10. *Hearings*, 884, 892, 1132-3, 1764, 2503, 3018-19.
11. *Hearings*, 355, 387, 599, 635, 692, 1514-22, 1533-4, 1615, 1933.
12. *Hearings*, 1185, 1189, 1518, 1603, 1619, 1725-7, 1754; cf. Acheson, *The Pattern of Responsibility*, 286-7.
13. *Hearings*, 1222-3.
14. Truman, op cit. Vol. II, 462-3; *Hearings*, 620.
15. *Hearings*, 1584; cf. *Hearings*, 1013-14, 1078-81, 1620, 1763.

16. *Hearings,* 23-4, 337, 619.
17. *Hearings,* 2741-2, 2958-74.
18. *Hearings,* 3190-92; cf. Spanier, op. cit. 12; Morgenthau, op. cit. 206ff.
19. *Hearings,* 74-84.
20. *Hearings,* 217.
21. *Hearings,* 53.
22. 'United States Foreign Policy for a Post-War Recovery Program,' Part II, 2041-2.
23. *Hearings,* 351-4, 669; cf. *Hearings,* 75-6, 385, 480-81.
24. *Hearings,* 1538-85.
25. *Hearings,* 1219; cf. *Hearings,* 1188, 1719-20.
26. *Hearings,* 733.
27. *Hearings,* 730-32; cf. Truman, op. cit. Vol. II, 380.
28. *Hearings,* 891; cf. Brodie, op. cit. 317.
29. 'Interlocking Subversion in Government Departments,' 2028-39; Gen. James A. Van Fleet, 'The Truth about Korea,' Part I, *Life* (New York, May 11, 1953), 127-32; Aron, op. cit. 31; 'The Korean War and Related Matters,' 17-20.
30. *Hearings before the Senate Committee on Armed Services,* 323.
31. *Hearings,* 732-3; cf. *Hearings,* 896.
32. *Hearings,* 366-7, 478-9, cf. *Hearings,* 1008; Acheson, *The Pattern of Responsibility,* 288-9.
33. *Hearings,* 1077, 1241, 1631.
34. *Hearings,* 1718-20.
35. *Hearings,* 898.
36. *Hearings,* 1440.
37. *Hearings,* 1613.
38. *Hearings,* 325, 1717; cf. *Hearings,* 177.
39. *Hearings,* 970-71, 1309; Huntington, op. cit. 384; Millis, op. cit. 333-58.
40. *Hearings,* 490, 1994.
41. Truman, op. cit. Vol. II, 382-3.
42. *Hearings,* 274, 3171ff.
43. *Hearings,* 1718-19; cf. *Hearings,* 1859-78, 1936, 2019.
44. *Hearings,* 482-4, 621-3, 687.
45. *Hearings,* 897-1069.
46. Truman, op. cit. Vol. II, 383; *Hearings,* 741, 1218.
47. *Hearings,* 1218-20.
48. *Hearings,* 1418, 3105.
49. *Hearings,* 1631-59.
50. *Hearings,* 644-6; cf. Kennan, *American Diplomacy 1900-1950,* 119.
51. *Hearings,* 219, 611-12, 956ff., 3196, 3278; see above Chap. X.
52. *Hearings,* 1945.
53. *Hearings,* 1226; cf. *Hearings,* 1278, 1470.
54. *Hearings,* 628-9, 952.

55. *Hearings,* 80.
56. *Hearings,* 366, cf. *Hearings,* 370, 732-3, 945-6; Osgood, op. cit. 192-3; Rovere and Schlesinger, op. cit. 280.
57. *Hearings,* 30, 68.
58. *Hearings,* 642-3.
59. *Hearings,* 30.
60. *Hearings,* 610.
61. Rovere and Schlesinger, op. cit. 98, 265, 279; cf. *Hearings,* 3547-52.
62. *Hearings,* 960-72; cf. *Hearings,* 1065.
63. Williams, loc. cit. 32ff.; Arthur Smith, *Old Fuss and Feathers* (New York, 1937), 253-4, 335-43; DeVoto, op. cit. 198ff.
64. *Hearings,* 955; cf. *Hearings,* 1716.
65. *Hearings,* 756.
66. *Hearings,* 898-9; cf. *Hearings,* 1224.
67. General of the Army Omar N. Bradley, *A Soldier's Story* (New York, 1951), 535. Of course Churchill's objectives usually embraced prestige factors, such as the capture of Rome in 1944, but by 1945 such objectives were justified.
68. *Hearings,* 1568; cf. *Hearings,* 1420.
69. *Hearings,* 1191, 1304, 1416-20, 1760.
70. *Hearings,* 1716ff.; cf. *Hearings,* 2085. An otherwise sympathetic critic, Raymond Aron, terms Acheson's 'success' a moral defeat, 'as [morally] the Chinese non-defeat was a victory.' Aron, op-cit. 27.
71. *Hearings,* 1761.
72. Donovan, op. cit. 117.
73. Ridgway, op. cit. 219-20; cf. *Hearings,* 492, 887, 3013; and Dille's similar argument that the 38th parallel constituted the best possible military line for the United States in Korea, Dille, op. cit. 78-9, as opposed to General Van Fleet's preference for the so-called northern neckline of Korea. 'Interlocking Subversion in Government Departments,' 2030.

CHAPTER XII. TRIUMPH AND TRAGEDY

1. Clark Tinch, 'Quasi-War Between Japan and the U.S.S.R., 1937-1939,' *World Politics* (Princeton, January 1951), 199.
2. Kissinger, *Nuclear Weapons and Foreign Policy,* 40.
3. Kennan, *American Diplomacy 1900-1950,* 73.
4. Karl von Clausewitz, *On War* (Washington, 1950), 20.
5. In General Kenney's affectionate characterization of MacArthur; Karig, op. cit. 142-3; cf. Clark and Henschel, op. cit. 96, 113.
6. Winston Churchill, *The Second World War, Vol. VI, Triumph and Tragedy* (Boston, 1953).
7. *Hearings,* 3585. See Brodie, op. cit. 312, for a definition of limited war.

8. Hanson W. Baldwin, 'Limited War,' *The Atlantic* (Boston, May 1959), 36-7; cf. Osgood, op. cit. 193.
9. A characteristic perception of an economist at war. Morgenstern, op. cit. 140-41.
10. *Hearings*, 2308; cf. *Hearings*, 895-6; Osgood, op cit. 182ff.; Kissinger, op. cit. 42-53; Morgenstern, op. cit. 146ff.
11. Forrestal, op. cit. 32; cf. *Hearings*, 1279; Kenney, op. cit. 244-5; Joy, op. cit. 176.
12. For a relatively recent Air Force expression of this view, see 'A Quarterly Review Staff Brief, Korea—An Opportunity Lost,' *Air University Quarterly Review* (Maxwell Air Force Base, Ala., Spring 1958), 25-7.

Bibliography

I. Bound Official and Semi-Official Sources, Congressional and Parliamentary Hearings and Debates

'Aid to Korea,' *Hearings before the House Committee on Foreign Affairs,* 81st Congress, 1st Session. U.S.G.P.O., Washington, 1949.

Airpower, The Decisive Weapon in Korea, edited by Col. James F. Stewart. Van Nostrand, Princeton, 1957.

'Assignment of Ground Forces of the United States to Duty in the European Area,' *Hearings before the Senate Committee on Foreign Relations and Armed Services,* 82d Congress, 1st Session. U.S.G.P.O., Washington, February 16, 1951.

Cagle, Comdr. M. C. and Manson, Comdr. F. A., *The Sea War in Korea.* United States Naval Institute, Annapolis, 1957.

Command Decisions by the Office of the Chief of Military History, Dept. of the Army, including articles by Martin Blumenson, Louis Morton, and Robert H. Smith. Harcourt Brace, New York, 1959.

Congressional Record. U.S.G.P.O., Washington, 1949-51.

'Extension in European Recovery,' *Hearings before the Senate Committee on Foreign Affairs,* 81st Congress, 2d Session. U.S.G.P.O., Washington, 1950.

Hearings before the Joint Committee on Investigation of the Pearl Harbor Attack, 79th Congress, 1st Session. U.S.G.P.O., Washington, 1946.

Hearings before the Senate Committee on Armed Services, 82d Congress, 2d Session. U.S.G.P.O., Washington, May 21, 1952.

Hearings before the Senate Subcommittee on Appropriations, 81st Congress, 2d Session. U.S.G.P.O., Washington, 1950.

House of Commons Debates. H.M.S.O., London, 1950-51.

'Interlocking Subversion in Government Departments,' *Hearings before the Senate Subcommittee on the Judiciary,* 83d Congress, 2d Session. U.S.G.P.O., Washington, 1952.

Karig, Capt. W., Cagle, Comdr. M. C., and Manson, Lt. Comdr. F. A., *Battle Report, The War in Korea,* prepared from official sources. Farrar and Rinehart, New York, 1952. Cited as Karig.

Matloff, Maurice, *United States Army in World War II, The War Department, Strategic Planning for Coalition Warfare 1943-1944.* Office of the Chief of Military History, Dept. of the Army, Washington, 1959.

Bibliography

'Military Situation in the Far East,' *Hearings before the Joint Senate Committee on Armed Services and Foreign Relations*, 82d Congress, 1st Session. U.S.G.P.O., Washington, 1951. Cited as *Hearings*, or in the event of possible confusion, as (MacArthur) *Hearings*.

Miller, John Jr., Carroll, O., and Tackley, M., *Korea 1951-1953*, Office of the Chief of Military History, Dept. of the Army. U.S.G.P.O., Washington, 1953.

Milner, Samuel, *United States Army in World War II, The War in the Pacific, Victory in Papua*, Office of the Chief of Military History, Dept. of the Army. U.S.G.P.O., Washington, 1957.

Montross, Lynn, and Canzona, Capt. Nicolas, *U.S. Marine Operations in Korea*, Historical Branch U.S. Marines HQ. U.S.G.P.O., Washington 1954-1957. Vol. I, *The Pusan Perimeter*, Vol. II, *The Inchon-Seoul Operation*, Vol. III, *The Chosin Reservoir Campaign*.

Morison, Samuel Eliot, *History of United States Naval Operations in World War II*. Little, Brown, Boston, 1948-58. Vol. I, *The Rising Sun in the Pacific*, Vol. XII, *Leyte, June 1944-January 1945*.

Morton, Louis, *United States Army in World War II, The War in the Pacific, The Fall of the Philippines*, Office of the Chief of Military History, Dept. of the Army. U.S.G.P.O., Washington, 1953.

'National Military Establishment Appropriation Bill for 1950,' *Hearings before the House Committee on Appropriations*, 81st Congress, 1st Session. U.S.G.P.O., Washington, 1949.

Odgers, George, *Australia in the War of 1939-1945, Air War Against Japan*. Australian War Memorial, Canberra, 1957.

Playfair, Maj. Gen. I.S.O., and others, *History of the Second World War. The Mediterranean and Middle East*, Vol. II. H.M.S.O., London, 1958.

Romanus, Charles, and Sunderland, Riley, *United States Army in World War II, China-India-Burma Theater, Time Runs Out*. Office of the Chief of Military History, Dept. of the Army, Washington, 1959.

State Department Bulletins. U.S.G.P.O., Washington, 1950-51.

Substance of Statements Made at Wake Island Conference. Compiled by General of the Army Omar N. Bradley from notes kept by the Conferees from Washington. Prepared for the Senate Armed Services and Foreign Relations Committees. U.S.G.P.O., Washington, 1951.

'The Korean War and Related Matters,' *Report of the Subcommittee on Internal Security to the Senate Judiciary Committee*, 84th Congress, 1st Session. U.S.G.P.O., Washington, January 21, 1955.

'The National Defense Program—Unification and Strategy,' *Hearings before the House Committee on Armed Services*. 81st Congress, 1st Session. U.S.G.P.O., Washington, 1949.

The War Reports of General of the Army George C. Marshall, H. H. Arnold and Fleet Admiral Ernest J. King. Lippincott, Philadelphia, 1947.

'United States Foreign Policy for a Post-war Recovery Program,' *Hearings before the House Committee on Foreign Affairs,* 80th Congress, 2d Session. U.S.G.P.O., Washington, March 3-10, 1948.

United States Policy in the Korean Conflict July 1950-February 1951, Dept. of State. U.S.G.P.O., Washington, 1951.

United States Relations with China with Special Reference to the Period 1944-1949, Dept. of State. U.S.G.P.O., Washington, 1949.

Watson, Mark, *United States Army in World War II, The War Department, Chief of Staff, Prewar Plans and Preparations,* Historical Division, Dept. of the Army. U.S.G.P.O., Washington, 1950.

What Happened at Pearl Harbor? Documents Pertaining to the Japanese Attack of December 7, 1941 and Its Background, edited by H. L. Trefousse. Twayne Publishers, New York, 1953.

II. AUTOBIOGRAPHY, DIARIES, MEMOIRS, AND PERSONAL RECORDS

Acheson, Dean, *The Pattern of Responsibility,* edited by McGeorge Bundy from the record of Secretary of State Dean Acheson. Houghton Mifflin, Boston, 1952.

Baille, Hugh, *High Tension.* Harper, New York, 1949.

Bradley, General of the Army Omar N., *A Soldier's Story.* Holt, New York, 1951.

Bryant, Sir Arthur, and Field Marshall Lord Alanbrooke, *Triumph in the West 1943-1946. Based on the Diaries and Autobiographical Notes of Field Marshall The Viscount Alanbrooke.* Collins, London, 1959.

Churchill, Winston, *The Second World War,* Vol. IV., *The Hinge of Fate,* Vol. V, *Closing the Ring,* Vol. VI, *Triumph and Tragedy.* Houghton Mifflin, Boston, 1950-53.

Clark, Gen. Mark W., *Calculated Risk.* Harper, New York, 1950.

———, *From the Danube to the Yalu.* Harper, New York, 1954.

Dean, Gen. William, *General Dean's Story,* as told to William Worden. Viking, New York, 1954.

Eden, Sir Anthony, *The Memoirs of the Right Honorable Sir Anthony Eden, Full Circle.* Houghton Mifflin, Boston, 1960.

Eichelberger, Gen. R. L., with Milton MacKaye, *Our Jungle Road to Tokyo.* Viking, New York, 1950.

Eisenhower, General of the Army Dwight D., *Crusade in Europe.* Doubleday, New York, 1948.

Forrestal, James, *The Forrestal Diaries,* edited by Walter Millis and E. S. Duffield. Viking, New York, 1951.

Joy, Adm. C. Turner, *How Communists Negotiate.* Macmillan, New York, 1955.

Kenney, Gen. George, *The MacArthur I Know.* Duell, Sloan and Pearce, New York, 1951.

Bibliography

Leahy, Fleet Adm. William, *I Was There, The Personal Story of the Chief of Staff to Presidents Roosevelt and Truman Based on His Notes and Diaries Made at the Time.* Whittlesey House, New York, 1950.

Lee, Clark, *One Last Look Around.* Duell, Sloan and Pearce, New York, 1947.

MacArthur on War, edited by Frank Waldrop. Duell, Sloan and Pearce, New York, 1942.

McClellan's Own Story, The War for the Union. Webster and Co., New York, 1887.

Pannikar, K. M., *In Two Chinas, Memoirs of a Diplomat.* Allen and Unwin, London, 1955.

Ridgway, Gen. Matthew B., *Soldier, The Memoirs of Matthew B. Ridgway,* as told to Harold Masters. Harper, New York, 1956.

Stimson, Henry, and Bundy, McGeorge, *On Active Service in Peace and War.* Harper, New York, 1947.

Taylor, Gen. Maxwell D., *The Uncertain Trumpet.* Harper, New York, 1960.

Truman, Harry S., *Memoirs by Harry S. Truman,* Vol. I, *Year of Decisions,* Vol. II, *Years of Trial and Hope.* Doubleday, New York, 1955-56.

——, *Mr. Citizen,* Bernard Geis Associates, New York, 1960.

Truman Speaks. Three Lectures at Columbia University, April 27-29, 1959, Harry S. Truman. Columbia University Press, New York, 1960.

The Private Papers of Senator Vandenberg, edited by Arthur Vandenberg, Jr., with V. A. Morris. Houghton Mifflin, Boston, 1952.

Wedemeyer, Gen. Albert C., *Wedemeyer Reports.* Holt, New York, 1948.

III. BIOGRAPHY

Churchill, Randolph S., *The Rise and Fall of Sir Anthony Eden,* Macgibbon and Kee, London, 1959.

Davis, Kenneth, *Soldier of Democracy, A Biography of Dwight D. Eisenhower.* Doubleday, New York, 1949.

Donovan, Robert, *Eisenhower, The Inside Story.* Harper, New York, 1956.

Driberg, Tom, *Guy Burgess, A Profile With Background.* London, 1956.

Dupuy, R. E., and Dupuy, T. N., *Brave Men and Great Captains.* Harper, New York, 1959.

——, *Men of West Point, The First 150 Years of the United States Military Academy.* Sloane, New York, 1951.

Frye, William, *Marshall, Citizen Soldier.* Bobbs-Merrill, New York, 1947.

Gunther, John, *The Riddle of MacArthur.* Harper, New York, 1951.

Hersey, John, *Men on Bataan.* Knopf, New York, 1943.

Hibbert, Christopher, *Wolfe at Quebec.* The World Publishing Co., New York, 1959.

Kelly, Frank, and Ryan, Cornelius, *MacArthur.* W. H. Allen, London, 1957.

Lee, Clark, and Henschel, Richard, *Douglas MacArthur*. Holt, New York, 1952.
Oliver, Robert T., *Syngman Rhee: The Man Behind the Myth*. Dodd Mead, New York, 1954.
Salvemini, Gaetano, *Mussolini, Diplomate*. Paris, 1932.
Sherwood, Robert, *Roosevelt and Hopkins, an Intimate History*. Harper, New York, 1948.
Smith, Arthur, *Old Fuss and Feathers, The Life and Exploits of Lieutenant General Winfield Scott*. The Keystone Press, New York, 1937.
Whitney, Maj. Gen. Courtney, *MacArthur, His Rendezvous with History*. Knopf, New York, 1956.
White, William S., *The Taft Story*. Harper, New York, 1954.
Williams, T. Harry, *Lincoln and His Generals*. Knopf, New York, 1952.
Willoughby, Maj. Gen. Charles and John Chamberlain, *MacArthur 1941-1951*. McGraw Hill, New York, 1954.

IV. PRESS AND PERIODICALS

In view of their great number, only the more important of this category of sources are cited with author's names or subtitles. All sources here thus are arranged alphabetically under publication only.

Air Force, Special Issue. Washington, March 1951.
Air University Quarterly Review. Maxwell Air Force Base, Ala., Spring 1957.
American Mercury. T. Harry Williams, "The Macs and the Ikes, America's Two Military Traditions.' New York, October 1952.
Army. Capt. Martin Blumenson, 'MacArthur's Divided Command.' Washington, November 1956.
Army. Lt. Col. James F. Schnabel, 'The Inchon Landing—Perilous Gamble or Exemplary Boldness?'. edited by Maj. B. C. Mossman. Washington, May 1959.
Cosmopolitan. Maj. Gen. Charles Willoughby, 'The Truth About Korea.' New York, December 1951.
Encounter. London, January, 1959.
Foreign Affairs. New York, October 1950, April 1951, April, October 1955, April, October 1956, January, October 1957; and *The Foreign Affairs Reader*, edited by H. F. Armstrong for the Council on Foreign Affairs. Harper, New York, 1947.
Harpers. Albert Warner, 'How the Korea Decision Was Made.' New York, June 1951.
Infantry Journal. Washington, January 1947.
Life. New York, December 8, 1941; May 19, 1952. Gen. James A. Van Fleet, 'The Truth about Korea,' May 11, 18, 1953; September 5, 1955; November 9, 1959; June 27, 1960.
Look. Robert Sherwood, 'The Feud Between Ike and Mac.' Des Moines, July 1, 1952; November 24, 1959.
Marine Corps Gazette. Quantico, November 1952; July 1953.

Bibliography

Military Affairs. Washington, Winter 1957, Autumn 1958.
Newsweek. New York, January 10, September 11, October 11, October 30, November 27, December 11, 1950.
Orbis. A. V. Cottrell and V. E. Dougherty, 'The Lessons of Korea and the Power of Men.' Philadelphia, Spring 1958.
The Army Quarterly. London, January 1958.
The Atlantic. Hanson W. Baldwin, 'Limited War' and others. Boston, May 1959.
The Christian Science Monitor. Boston, June 26, 1950.
The Contemporary Review. London, November 1953.
The New Republic. Richard Rovere, 'The Evil Conspiracy Against General MacArthur.' New York, April 9, 1956.
The New York Herald Tribune. Paris, September 13, 1958; June 27, 1960.
The New York Times. New York, March 2, June 6, 1949; September 1, 15, October 31, November 29, December 1, 5, 6, 7, 1950; January 5, 6, 1951; February 1, 1953; May 1, December 4, 1956; March 20, November 23, 1957; January 12, February 10, September 12, November 9, 1958; February 8, March 9, 31, April 17, November 29, 1959.
The Reporter. New York, August 1, 29, 1950; January 23, 1951; January 8, August 19, 1952; March 3, 1953; February 5, November 4, 18, 1954; February 5, March 19, 1959; February 18, 1960.
The Saturday Evening Post. Philadelphia, May 27, 1947; Beverly Smith, 'Why We Went to War in Korea,' November 10, 1951.
The Washington Post. Washington, June 27, 1950; July 22, 1959.
The Yale Review. New Haven, Summer 1951; Summer 1954.
Time. New York, June 13, 1949; August 28, September 18, 1950; November 3, 1952; January 12, February 12, December 14, 1959.
United States Naval Institute Proceedings. Annapolis, March 1952, November 1954; July, November 1955; April 1957; February 1958; Comdr. M. C. Cagle, 'Errors of the Korean War,' March 1958.
United States News and World Report. Washington, December 8, 15, 1950; September 14, 1954; General of the Army Douglas MacArthur, 'Mr. Truman Yielded to Counsels of Fear,' February 17, 1956; John P. Sutherland, 'The Story Gen. Marshall Told Me,' November 2, 1959.
World Politics. Princeton, January 1951, January 1954; Alexander George, 'American Policy-Making and North Korean Aggression,' January 1955; Louis Morton, 'Historia Mentem Armet: Lessons of the Past,' January 1960.

V. BOUND SECONDARY SOURCES

Acheson, Dean, *Power and Diplomacy.* Harvard University Press, Cambridge, 1958.
Aron, Raymond, *On War.* Doubleday, Garden City, 1959.
———, *The Century of Total War.* Beacon Books, Boston, 1955.

218

Ballantine, Joseph W., *Formosa, A Problem for United States Foreign Policy.* The Brookings Institution, Washington, 1952.

Berger, Carl, *The Korean Knot, A Military-Political History.* University of Pennsylvania Press, Philadelphia, 1957.

Braisted, W. R., *The United States Navy in the Pacific 1897-1909.* University of Texas Press, Austin, 1958.

Brodie, Bernard, *Strategy in the Missile Age.* The Rand Corporation, Princeton University Press, Princeton, 1959.

Chiang Kai-shek, *Soviet Russia in China, A Summing-Up at Seventy.* Farrar, Straus and Cudahy, New York, 1958.

Clausewitz, Karl von, *On War.* Infantry Journal Press, Washington, 1950.

Craig, Gordon C., *The Politics of the Prussian Army 1640-1945.* The Clarendon Press, Oxford, 1955.

De Gaulle, Gen. Charles, *The Edge of the Sword.* Criterion Books, New York, 1960.

DeVoto, Bernard, *The Year of Decision.* Little, Brown, Boston, 1943.

Dille, John, *Substitute for Victory.* Doubleday, Garden City, 1954.

Dupuy, R. E., and Dupuy, T. N., *Military Heritage of America.* McGraw Hill, New York, 1956.

Eyre, James, Jr., *The Roosevelt-MacArthur Conflict.* Chambersburg, Pennsylvania.

Feis, Herbert, *The China Tangle, The American Effort in China From Pearl Harbor to the Marshall Mission.* Princeton University Press, Princeton, 1953.

Garthoff, Raymond, *Soviet Strategy in the Nuclear Age.* Praeger, New York, 1958.

Gavin, Lt. Gen. James M., *War and Peace in the Space Age.* Harper, New York, 1958.

Goodrich, L. M., *Korea, A Study of U.S. Policy in the United Nations.* Council on Foreign Relations, New York, 1956.

Griswold, A. Whitney, *The Far Eastern Policy of the United States.* Harcourt Brace, New York, 1938.

Hilsman, Roger, *Strategic Intelligence and National Decisions.* The Free Press, Glencoe, Ill., 1956.

Huntington, Samuel B., *The Soldier and the State, The Theory and Politics of Civil-Military Relations.* Harvard University, Cambridge, 1957.

Janowitz, Morris, *The Professional Soldier, A Social and Political Portrait.* The Free Press, Glencoe, Ill., 1960.

Kennan, George F., *American Diplomacy 1900-1950.* University of Chicago Press, Chicago, 1951.

———, *Realities of American Foreign Policy.* Princeton University Press, Princeton, 1954.

Kinkaid, Eugene, *In Every War but One.* W. W. Norton, New York, 1959.

Kissinger, Henry A., *A World Restored: Metternich, Castlereagh, and the Problems of Peace, 1812-1822.* Houghton Mifflin, Boston, 1951.

Bibliography

Kissinger, Henry A., *Nuclear Weapons and Foreign Policy*. Council on Foreign Relations, Harper, New York, 1957.

Leech, Margaret, *In the Days of McKinley*. Harper, New York, 1959.

Leites, Nathan, *A Study of Bolshevism*. The Free Press, Glencoe, Ill., 1953.

Liu, F. F., *A Military History of Modern China, 1942-1949*. Princeton University Press, Princeton, 1956.

MacDonald, Dwight, *Memoirs of a Revolutionist, Essays in Political Criticism*. Farrar, Straus and Young, New York, 1957.

Mahan, Capt. Alfred T., *The Influence of Sea Power upon the French Revolution and Empire*, Vols. I-II. Little Brown, Boston, 1897.

Mao Tse-tung, *Imperialism and All Reactionaries are Paper Tigers*. Foreign Language Press, Peking, 1958.

———, *Selected Works*, Vols. I-IV. Lawrence and Wishart, London, 1954.

Marshall, Brig. Gen. S. L. A., *The River and the Gauntlet, Defeat of the Eighth Army by Chinese Communist Forces, November 1950*. William Morrow, New York, 1953.

Millis, Walter, *Arms and Men, A Study in American Military History*. Putnam, New York, 1956.

——— with Harvey Mansfield and Harold Stein, *Arms and the State, Civil-Military Elements in National Policy*. The Twentieth Century Fund, New York, 1958. Cited as Millis.

Morgenstern, Oskar, *The Question of National Defense*. Random House, New York, 1959.

Morgenthau, Hans J., *In Defense of the National Interest, A Critical Examination of American Foreign Policy*. Knopf, New York, 1951.

North, Robert G., *Moscow and Chinese Communists*. Stamford University Press, Stamford, 1953.

Oliver, Robert, *Why War Came to Korea*. Fordham University Press, New York, 1950.

Osgood, R. E., *Limited War, The Challenge to American Strategy*. University of Chicago Press, Chicago, 1957.

Poats, Rutherford, *Decision in Korea*. MacBride, New York, 1954.

Ransom, H. H., *Central Intelligence and National Security*. Harvard University Press, Cambridge, 1958.

Rigg, Lt. Col. Robert, *Red China's Fighting Hordes*. The Military Service Publishing Co., Harrisburg, Pa., 1951.

Rostow, W. W., and others, *The Prospects for Communist China*. Massachusetts Institute of Technology, Cambridge, 1954.

Rovere, Richard, and Schlesinger, Arthur, Jr., *The General and the President and the Future of American Foreign Policy*. Farrar, Straus and Young, New York, 1951.

Sapin, Burton M. and Snyder, Richard C., *The Role of the Military in American Foreign Policy*. Doubleday, Garden City, N. Y., 1954.

Soldiers and Governments, Nine Studies in Civil and Military Relations, edited by Michael Howard. Eyre and Spottiswood. London, 1957.

Spanier, John W., *The Truman-MacArthur Controversy and the Korean War.* Harvard University Press, Cambridge, 1959.
Stacey, C. P., *Quebec 1759, The Siege and the Battle.* St. Martin's Press, New York, 1959.
Stebbins, Richard, *The United States in World Affairs.* Council on Foreign Relations, Harper, New York, 1951.
Strausz-Hupé, R., Kintner, W. R., Dougherty, J. E., and Cottrell, A. V., *Protracted Conflict.* A Foreign Policy Research Institute Book, Harper, New York, 1959.
Taft, Robert A., *A Foreign Policy for Americans.* Doubleday, New York, 1951.
Vagts, Alfred, *A History of Militarism, Romance and Realities of a Profession.* W. W. Norton, New York, 1937.
———, *Defense and Diplomacy, The Soldier and the Conduct of Foreign Relations.* Kings Crown Press, New York, 1956.
Walker, Richard L., *China Under Communism, The First Five Years.* Yale University Press, New Haven, 1955.
———, *The Continuing Struggle, Communist China and the Free World.* Athens Press, New York, 1958.

VI. MANUSCRIPTS AND MONOGRAPHS

Civil-Military Relations, An Annotated Bibliography 1940-1952. Prepared for the Social Science Research Council. Columbia University Press, New York, 1954.
Kaufman, William, *Policy Objectives and Military Action in the Korean War.* The Rand Corporation, Santa Monica, June 26, 1956.
Kecskemeti, Paul, *Strategic Surrender, The Politics of Victory and Defeat.* Rand Corporation MS, Santa Monica, Calif., July 26, 1957.
Lichterman, Martin, *To the Yalu and Back.* MS study for the Twentieth Century Fund under Harold Stein, Princeton, undated.
Mason, Bayley F., *The War in Korea, A Case Study in the Problems of Limited War.* Harvard University Defense Policy MS, Cambridge, Mass., October 1, 1956.
Paige, Glenn, *The United States Decision to Repel Aggression in Korea.* Foreign Policy Analysis Project MS, Northwestern University, August 1, 1956.
Pershing, General of the Armies John J., MS Papers in Library of Congress, Washington.
Ransome, H. R., 'The Politics of Air Power: A Comparative Analysis,' *Public Policy,* A Yearbook of the Harvard Graduate School of Business Administration, Cambridge, 1958.
Schnabel, Maj. James, 'Drive to the Yalu.' *Command Decision #25* MS in the Office of the Chief of Military History, Dept. of the Army, Washington, undated.
The Entry of the Soviet Union into the War Against Japan. Military Plans 1941-1945. Dept. of Defense Monograph prepared from official sources. U.S.G.P.O., Washington, September 1955.

Index

Index

Index